STICKMEN'S GUIDE TO EARTH— UNCOVERED

by Catherine Chambers
Illustrated by John Paul de Quay

Contents

Planet Earth—Uncovered	5	**Cities**	48
The Sky	6	On Top of the World	50
High in the Exosphere	8	Fun at the Top	52
Satellites in the Exosphere	10	Going Down	54
Floating in the Thermosphere	12	High Power	56
Looking into Space	14	On the Streets	58
Bright Lights in the Mesosphere	16	Power Under Our Feet	60
The Calm Stratosphere	18	Keeping Clean	62
The Ozone Layer	20	Travel Below Ground	64
Earth's Troposphere	22	Down Under	66
Storms and Twisters	24		
What's the Weather Like?	26	**Oceans**	68
		The Sunlight Zone	70
Mountains and Valleys	28	Superhighway	72
Snowy Peaks	30	Twilight Zone	74
Tough Alpine Life	32	Exploring the Seabed	76
Forested Slopes	34	The Midnight Zone	78
On the Plains	36	Deep-Sea Discoveries	80
The Valley Floor	38	The Black Abyss	82
Deep in the Canyon	40	Secrets of the Abyss	84
Down the Mine	42	The Ocean's Trenches	86
Volcano Power	44	Taking the Plunge	88
Smashing Plates	46	The Center of Earth	90
		Index	92

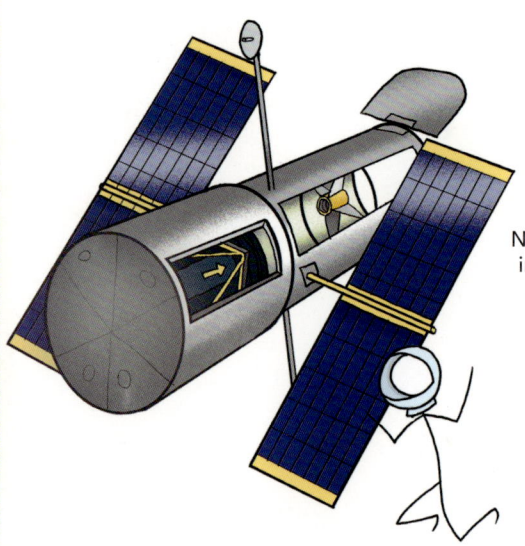

First published in 2020 by Hungry Tomato Ltd
F1, Old Bakery Studios, Blewetts Wharf,
Malpas Road, Truro,
Cornwall, TR1 1QH, UK

Copyright © 2020 Hungry Tomato Ltd

No part of this publication may be reproduced, stored in a retrieval system, or transmitted in any form or by any means, electronic, mechanical, photocopying, recording, or otherwise, without the prior written permission of the copyright owner.

A CIP catalogue record for this book is available from the British Library.

ISBN 978-1-913077-709

Printed and bound in China

Discover more at
www.mybeetlebooks.com

BEETLE BOOKS

Planet Earth—Uncovered

Welcome to Earth, as you have never seen it before. Follow the stickmen as they travel from the edge of Earth's atmosphere, 375 miles (600 km) above the ground, to its center, 36,000 feet (11,000 m) below our feet. On this journey, the stickmen will uncover Earth layer by layer. Whether it be giant squids in our oceans, exploding volcanoes, or walking cucumbers, be prepared to be amazed as the stickmen show a new side to our great planet.

The Sky

When we look up at the sky, we are looking through layers of gases called the atmosphere. These layers wrap around Earth like a pile of blankets, some thick and others thin. Each layer is made of a mixture of gases, covers a range of temperature and air pressure, and has a different effect on the way we live on Earth.

Exosphere
From around 375 miles (600 km)
Pressure is extremely low and gases are thin, with some escaping into space. Most satellites orbit Earth here.

Thermosphere
53 to 375 miles (85-600 km)
Gases are still thin, pressure is low, and the temperature increases with height. Bright colored lights pulsate.

Mesosphere
30 to 53 miles (50-85 km)
Temperatures are cold. Meteors shoot through and burn up. The highest clouds put on a light show over the poles.

Stratosphere
Minimum 4 to 30 miles (6-50 km)
The tips of Earth's highest clouds reach here. A layer of ozone gases protects Earth from the Sun's harmful rays.

Troposphere
0 to 12 miles (0-20 km) maximum
We can breathe oxygen and plants use carbon dioxide to grow. The boundary with the stratosphere is variable.

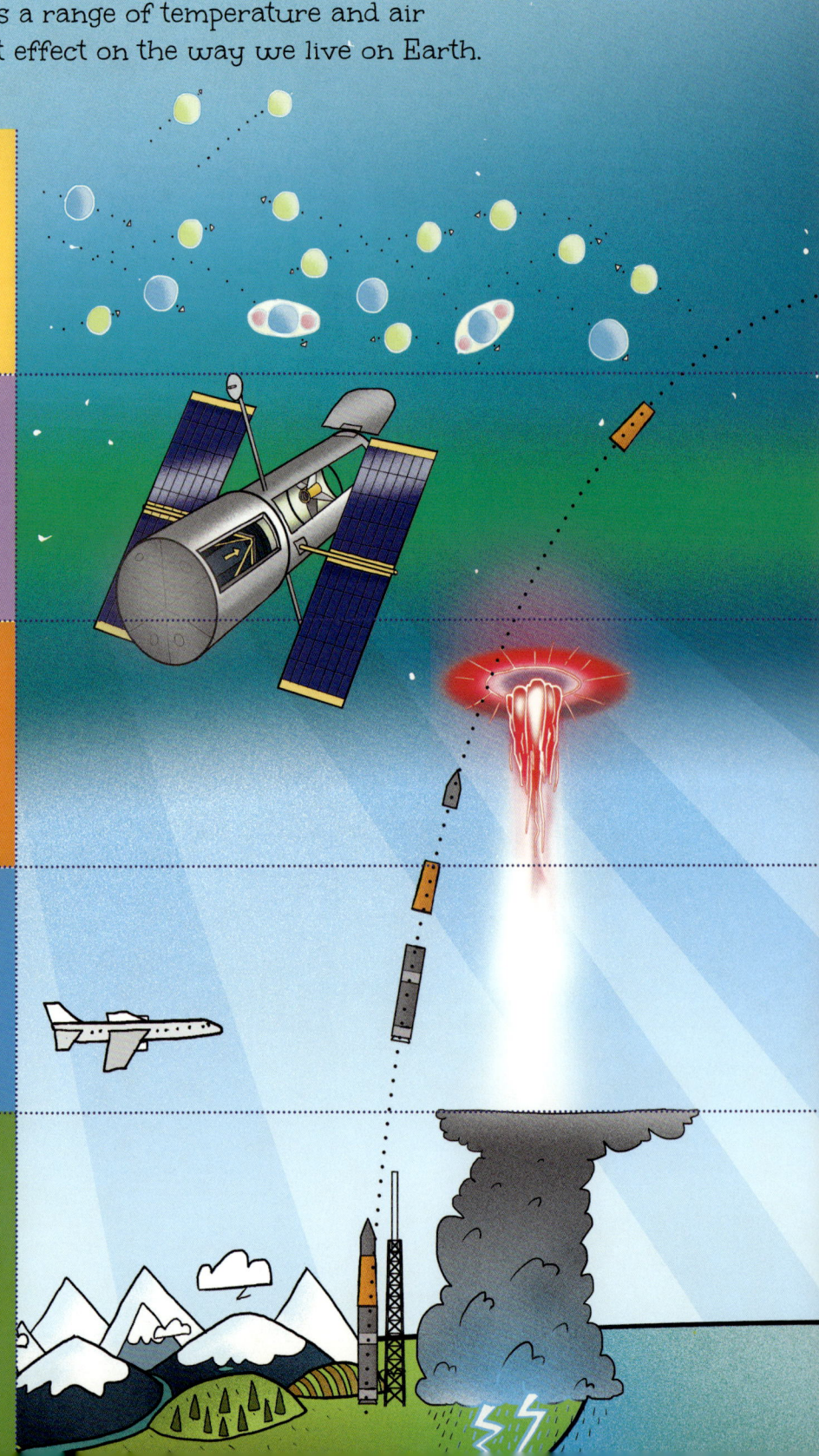

7

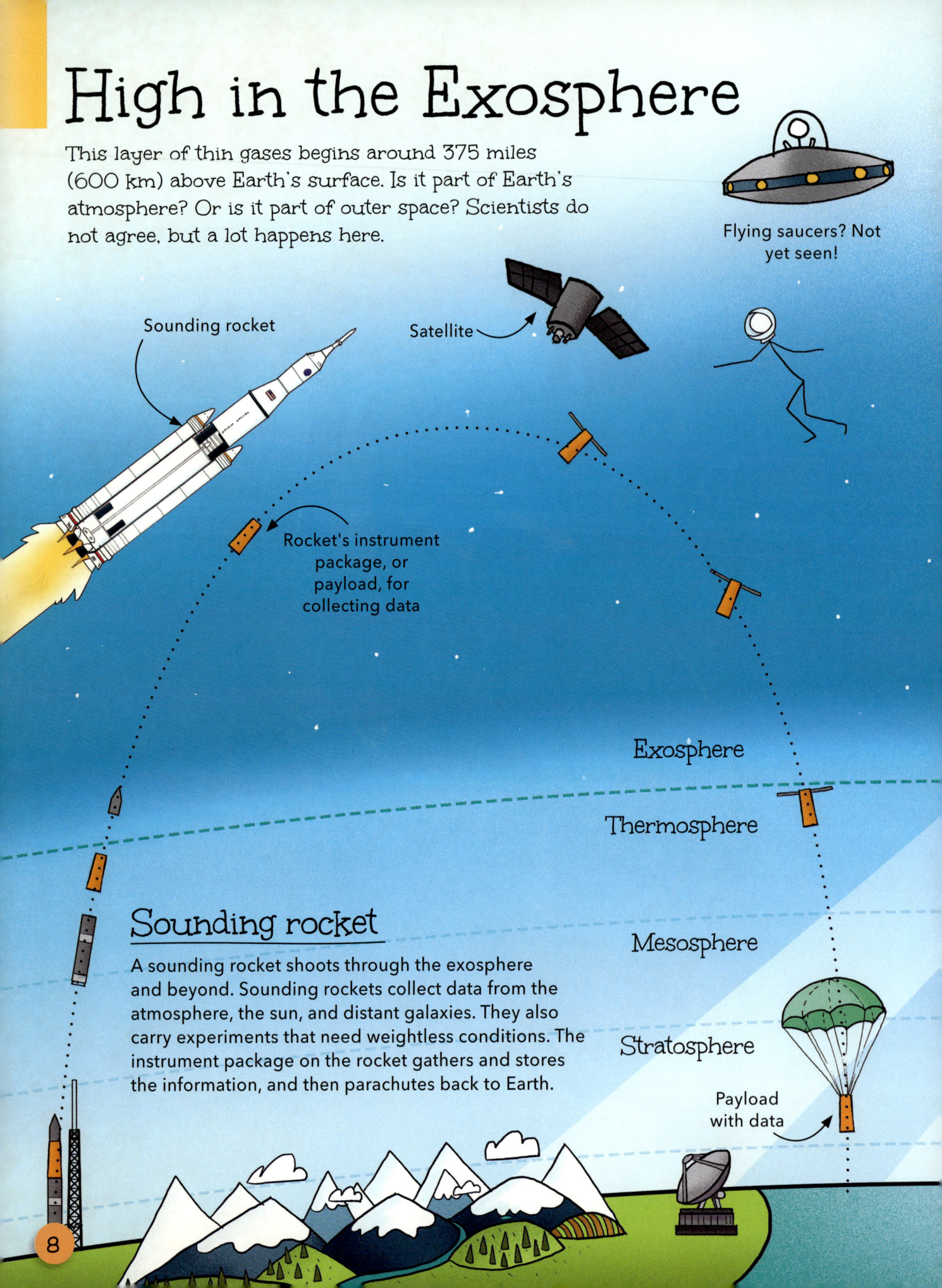

High in the Exosphere

This layer of thin gases begins around 375 miles (600 km) above Earth's surface. Is it part of Earth's atmosphere? Or is it part of outer space? Scientists do not agree, but a lot happens here.

Flying saucers? Not yet seen!

Sounding rocket

Satellite

Rocket's instrument package, or payload, for collecting data

Exosphere

Thermosphere

Mesosphere

Stratosphere

Payload with data

Sounding rocket

A sounding rocket shoots through the exosphere and beyond. Sounding rockets collect data from the atmosphere, the sun, and distant galaxies. They also carry experiments that need weightless conditions. The instrument package on the rocket gathers and stores the information, and then parachutes back to Earth.

Power of the sun

The sun is an active, searing-hot star that radiates energy toward Earth. At times, the sun emits strong blasts of ultraviolet, or UV, rays (found beyond the violet end of the light spectrum), as shown here, and X-rays. These make the thermosphere below bulge up into the exosphere. The boundary between these layers is never exact, but it is more stable at some times than others.

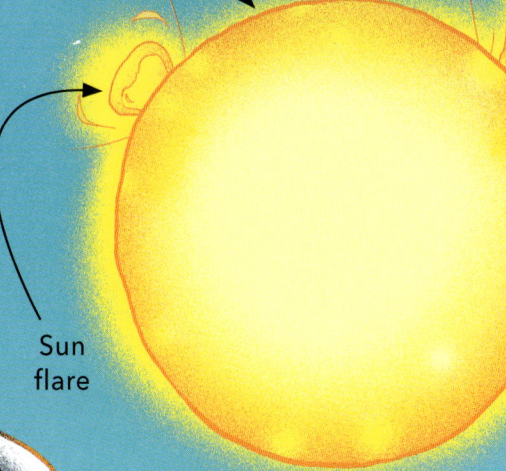

Sun flare

Hydrogen atom

On the way to the moon

The upper edge of the exosphere marks the end of Earth's atmosphere and the beginning of space. It is also halfway to the moon.

Helium atom

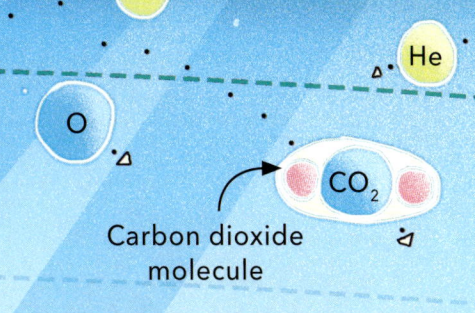

Carbon dioxide molecule

Oxygen atom

Glowing exosphere

Pictures of Earth taken with a UV telescope show the exosphere glowing. This eerie light is called the geocorona. It is created by the sun's UV rays reflecting off the cloud of hydrogen atoms surrounding Earth.

Speedy gases

The exosphere's gases are mainly hydrogen atoms, with some helium and carbon dioxide. There are some oxygen atoms, too. These gases speed along curved paths, without colliding. Earth's gravity pulls down most of them toward the troposphere, but the fastest zoom off into space.

Troposphere

Satellites in the Exosphere

About 2,000 artificial satellites orbit our planet at a height of about 12,400 miles (20,000 km) and above. They relay data, communication signals, or images to Earth by means of antennas and use solar power. They operate in the exosphere where they are safe from atmospheric drag, which would make them spiral down and burn up.

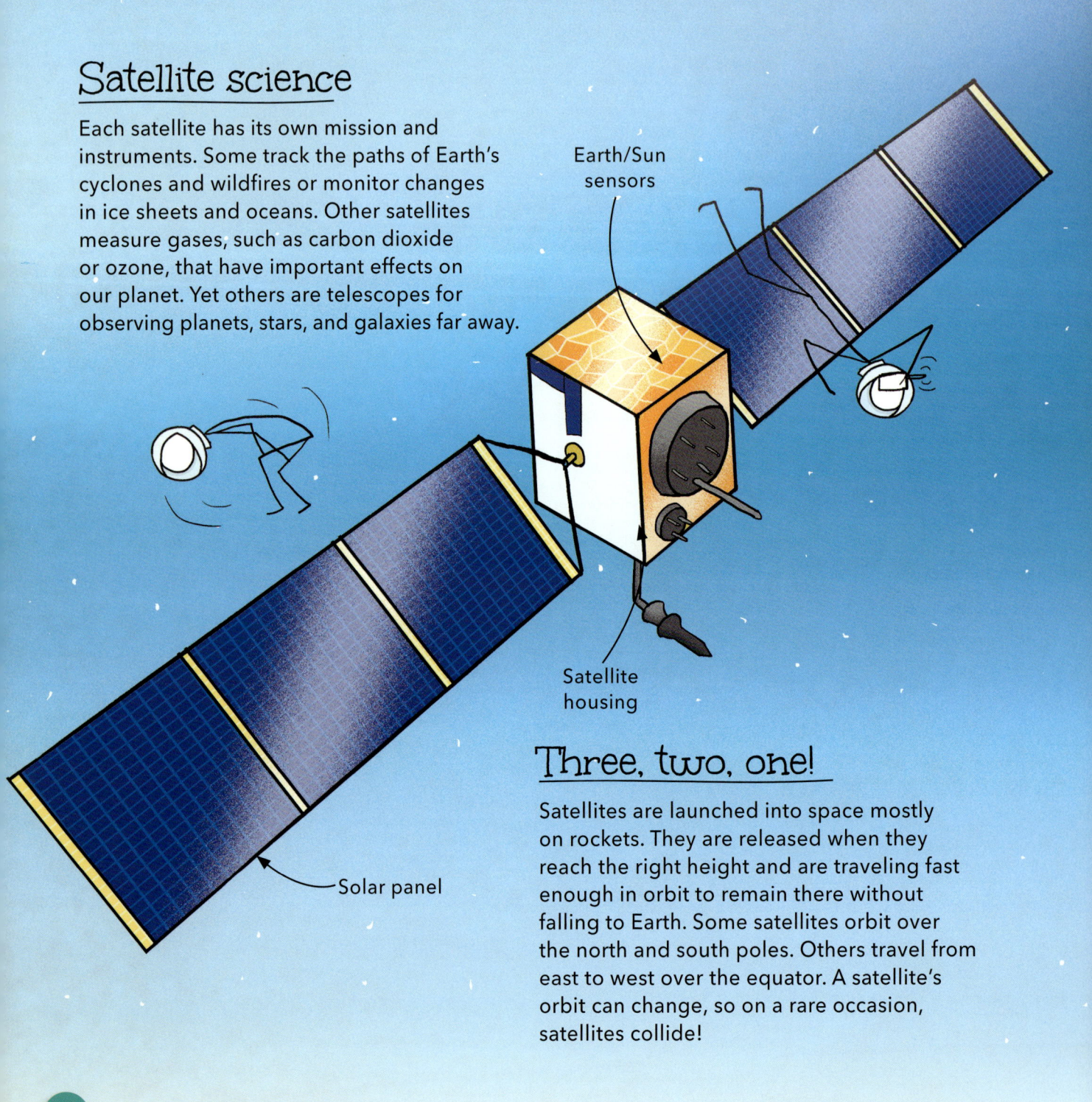

Satellite science

Each satellite has its own mission and instruments. Some track the paths of Earth's cyclones and wildfires or monitor changes in ice sheets and oceans. Other satellites measure gases, such as carbon dioxide or ozone, that have important effects on our planet. Yet others are telescopes for observing planets, stars, and galaxies far away.

Earth/Sun sensors

Satellite housing

Solar panel

Three, two, one!

Satellites are launched into space mostly on rockets. They are released when they reach the right height and are traveling fast enough in orbit to remain there without falling to Earth. Some satellites orbit over the north and south poles. Others travel from east to west over the equator. A satellite's orbit can change, so on a rare occasion, satellites collide!

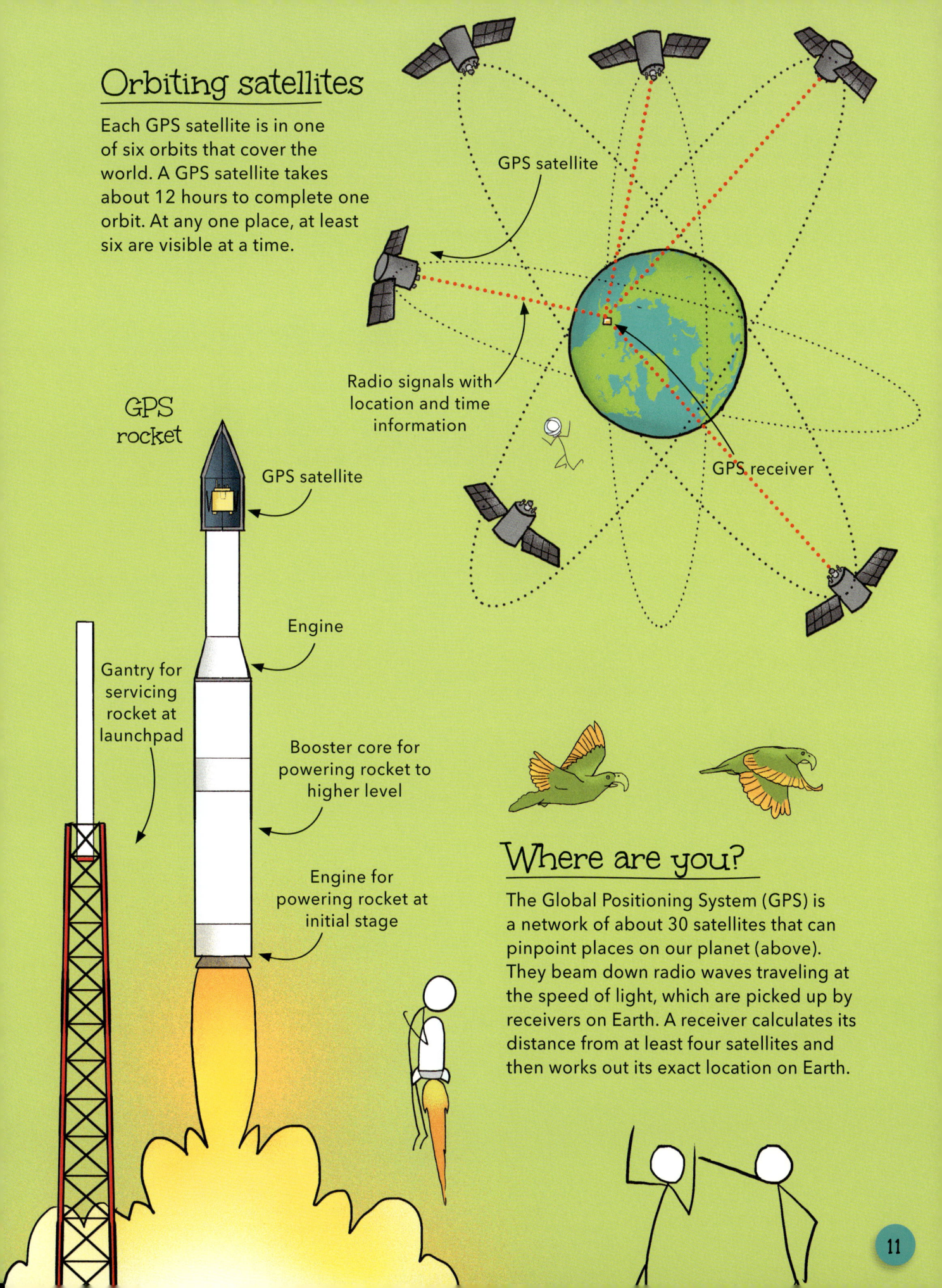

Orbiting satellites

Each GPS satellite is in one of six orbits that cover the world. A GPS satellite takes about 12 hours to complete one orbit. At any one place, at least six are visible at a time.

GPS satellite

Radio signals with location and time information

GPS receiver

GPS rocket

GPS satellite

Engine

Gantry for servicing rocket at launchpad

Booster core for powering rocket to higher level

Engine for powering rocket at initial stage

Where are you?

The Global Positioning System (GPS) is a network of about 30 satellites that can pinpoint places on our planet (above). They beam down radio waves traveling at the speed of light, which are picked up by receivers on Earth. A receiver calculates its distance from at least four satellites and then works out its exact location on Earth.

Floating in the Thermosphere

The deep thermosphere layer reaches from around 53 miles (85 km) to 375 miles (600 km) above Earth. Its main gas is nitrogen, with some oxygen, helium, and hydrogen. Toward the bottom of this layer, temperature falls and gravity's pull is stronger.

Working together

The International Space Station (ISS) is the largest artificial object put into space. It orbits 200 miles (320 km) above Earth, 16 times each day. A total of 15 countries cooperated to build ISS, and astronauts from those countries spend months on board, conducting scientific experiments. The weightlessness of space brings scientific results that can be helpful to us on Earth. You can track the ISS in real time online.

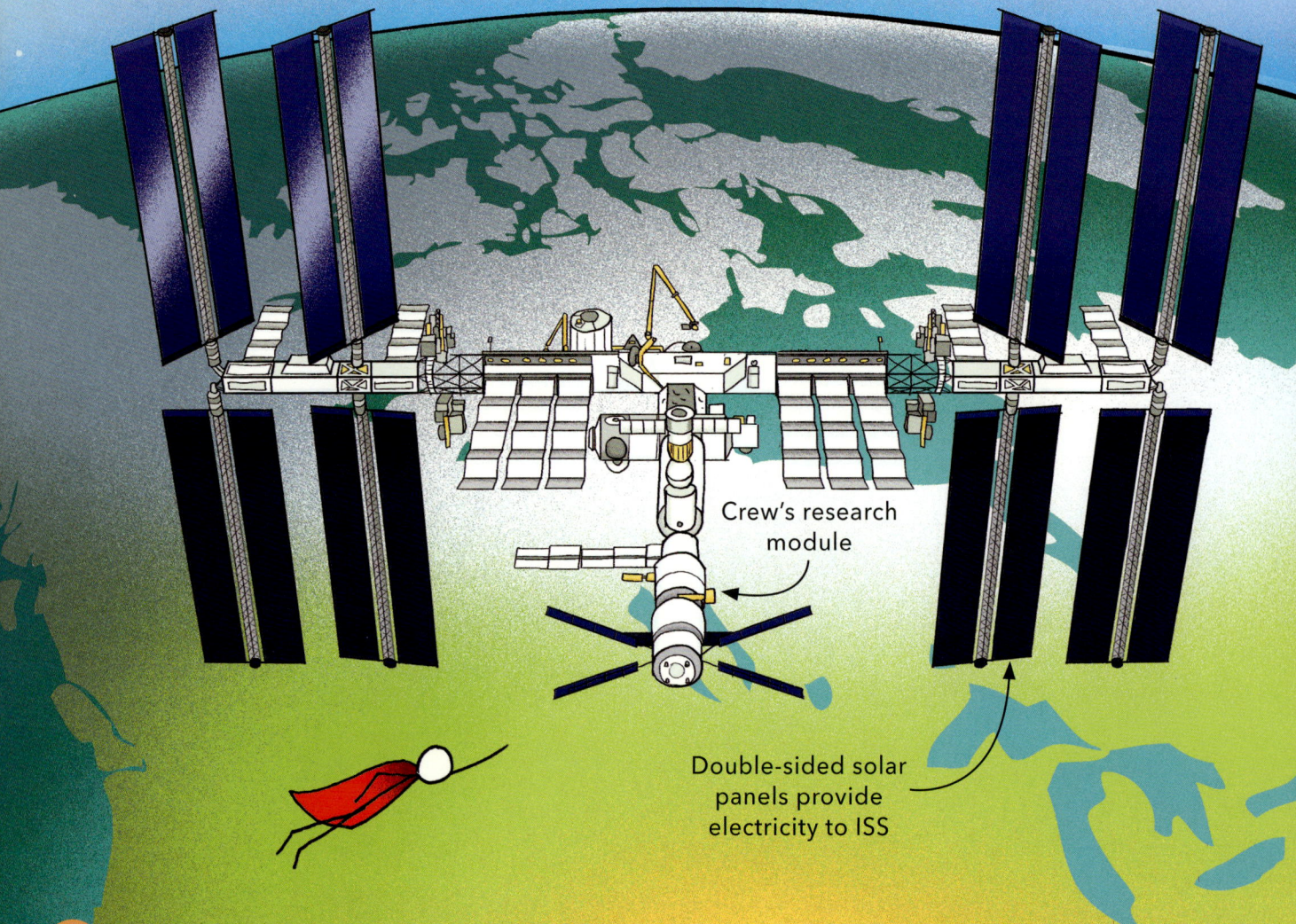

Crew's research module

Double-sided solar panels provide electricity to ISS

Amazing astronauts

Astronauts are scientists and engineers trained to work inside and outside space vehicles. A spacewalk today usually lasts between five and eight hours, depending on the job to be done. Astronauts are tethered to the spacecraft to prevent them from floating away, and they have a backpack with small jet thrusters so they can move around in space.

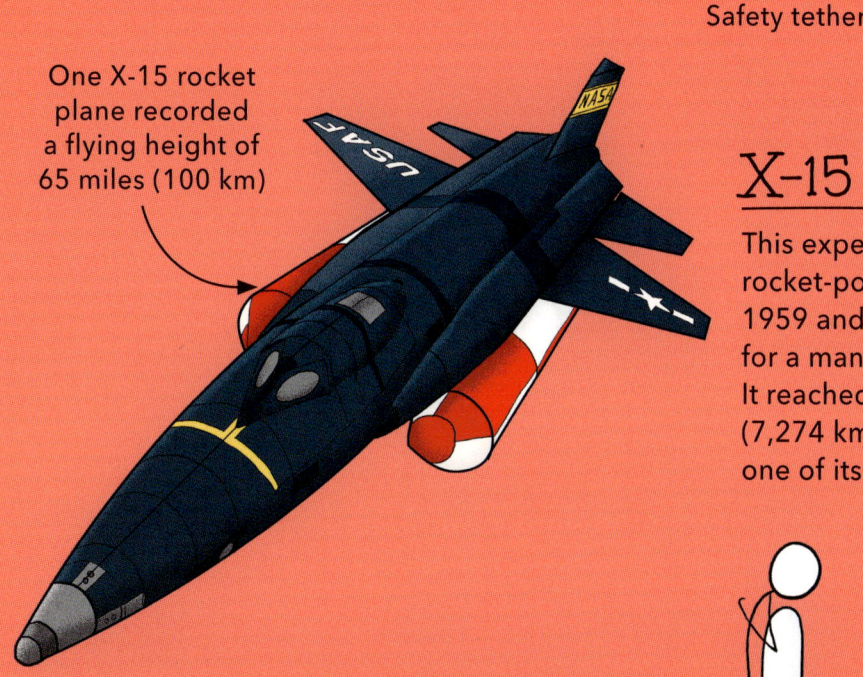

Oxygen line

Safety tether

One X-15 rocket plane recorded a flying height of 65 miles (100 km)

X-15 rocket plane

This experimental, hypersonic rocket-powered aircraft first flew in 1959 and still holds the speed record for a manned, powered aircraft. It reached 4,520 miles per hour (7,274 km/h) and Neil Armstrong was one of its pilots.

Super space shuttle

The space shuttle, in operation from 1982 to 2011, was the only manned, winged aircraft that could move into orbit and back again, returning its crew and payload. Its robotic arm, the Canadarm, was used to fix the ISS. It also took hold of the Hubble Space Telescope (see page 14) so that repairs could be made.

External fuel tank

Two rocket boosters provide 71 percent of thrust needed for launch

Orbiter (the only shuttle component that goes into orbit)

Looking into Space

The Hubble Space Telescope orbits Earth in the thermosphere at about 340 miles (547 km) above Earth. For more than 25 years, it has beamed back spectacular images of space, including planets, comets, exploding stars, nebulae (gas and dust clouds), and galaxies. Scientists use Hubble's data and images to learn more about these objects and the whole universe.

Through the telescope

Hubble captures its amazing images using both visible light and radiation we cannot see—ultraviolet and infrared—at each end of the light spectrum. It has five different instruments with cameras for taking particular kinds of images. Some of them can split light into its different wavelengths and some take pictures through special filters.

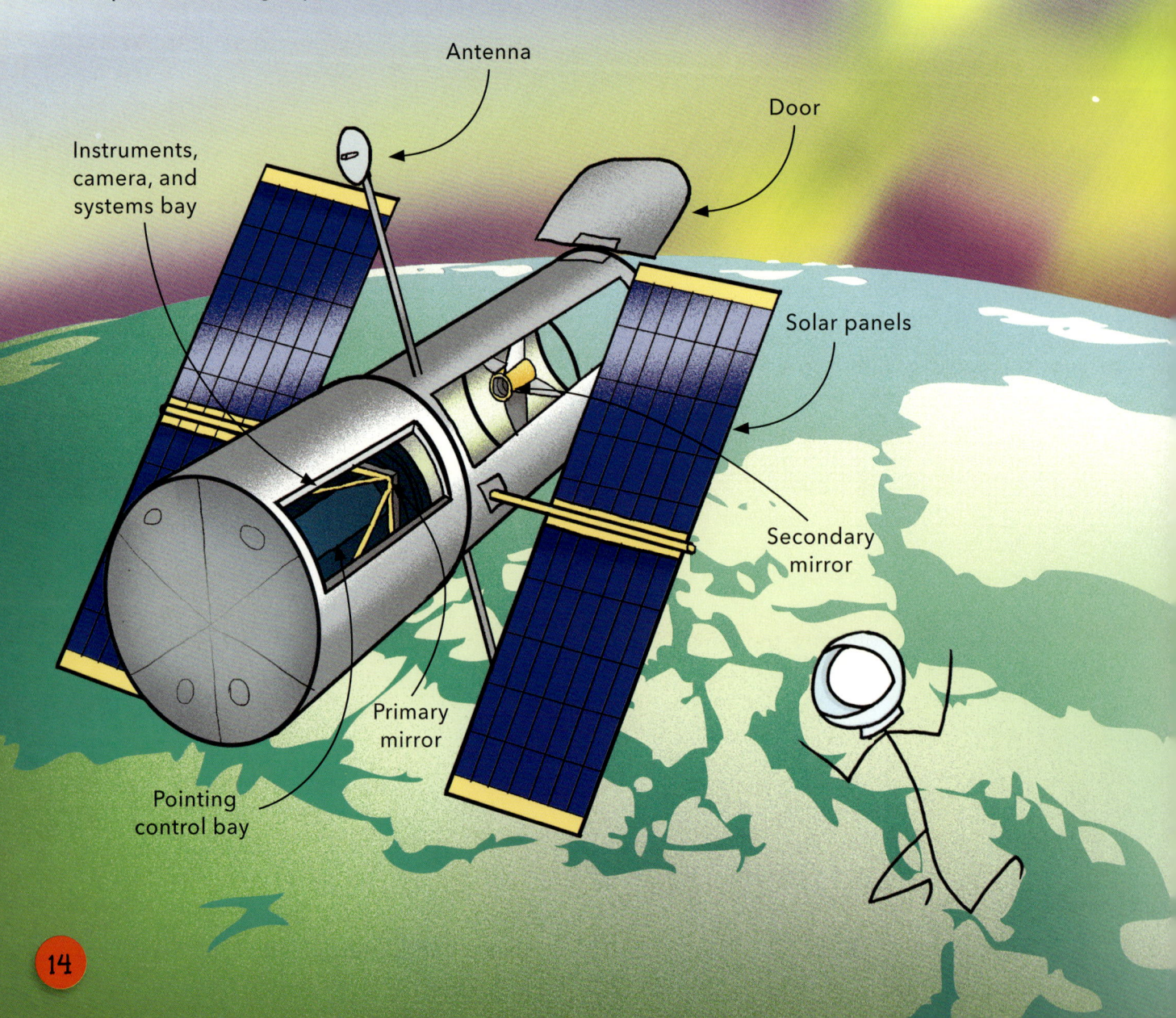

Antenna

Door

Instruments, camera, and systems bay

Solar panels

Secondary mirror

Primary mirror

Pointing control bay

Southern Pinwheel

This is Hubble's view of a spiral galaxy, nicknamed the Southern Pinwheel, in the constellation Hydra. Lying 15 million light-years away, it is relatively near and easier to see. The swirling blues and pinks are glowing gas where stars are being born. Among the thousands of star clusters and individual stars in this galaxy are supernova remnants—traces of giant stars that have exploded and died.

Pictures in the dark

Hubble has no flashlight to take images in the darkness of space. Instead, it aims and fixes onto its target with its Pointing Control System, which uses three special instruments called Fine Guidance Sensors. Then, its primary mirror captures and concentrates the light from space, reflecting it onto a smaller secondary mirror. This mirror focuses the light onto one of the cameras or instruments.

Bright Lights in the Mesosphere

The mesosphere is a thin layer of mixed gases around 30 miles (50 km) to 53 miles (85 km) above Earth. With fewer air molecules to absorb the sun's radiation, temperatures near the upper mesosphere plunge to –130°F (–90°C), the coldest in our atmosphere. Meteors shoot into this layer and then burn up.

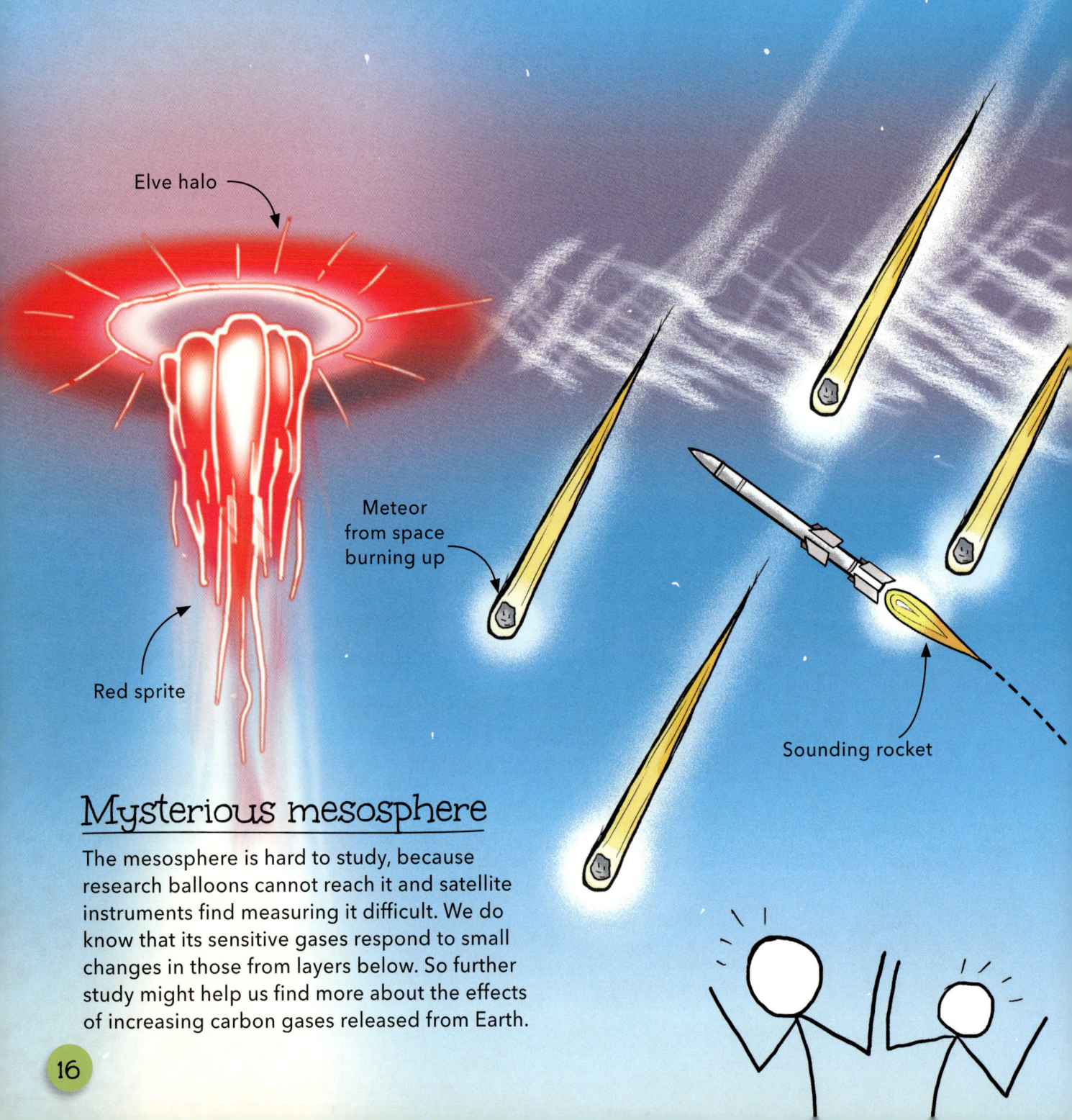

Elve halo

Meteor from space burning up

Red sprite

Sounding rocket

Mysterious mesosphere

The mesosphere is hard to study, because research balloons cannot reach it and satellite instruments find measuring it difficult. We do know that its sensitive gases respond to small changes in those from layers below. So further study might help us find more about the effects of increasing carbon gases released from Earth.

Night clouds

High night clouds, known as noctilucent clouds, occasionally illuminate the sky in the mesosphere, near Earth's poles. They are made of ice crystals that scatter light, making them shine. They occur in the freezing upper limit of this layer and are also known as polar mesospheric clouds.

Night cloud

Red sprites and elves

Long streaks of faint red light flash briefly above heavy storm clouds and lightning from the troposphere way below. A halo-shaped glow, or elve, forms above it (left). We do not know exactly why they form, but these fascinating lights are captured best by sensitive, low-light-level television (LLLTV) equipment.

Lightning storm

Airglow

The upper layers of the atmosphere give out faint light the whole time. This is called airglow. Looking edge on through the atmosphere from space, it makes a glowing band. Airglow is mostly caused by particles and radiation from the sun affecting gases in the atmosphere in different ways.

Airglow

The Calm Stratosphere

The stratosphere can reach down to around 4 miles (6 km) and rise to its highest point of around 30 miles (50 km) above Earth. These boundaries depend on the seasons and where you are in the world. They are also affected by electric storms in the troposphere below.

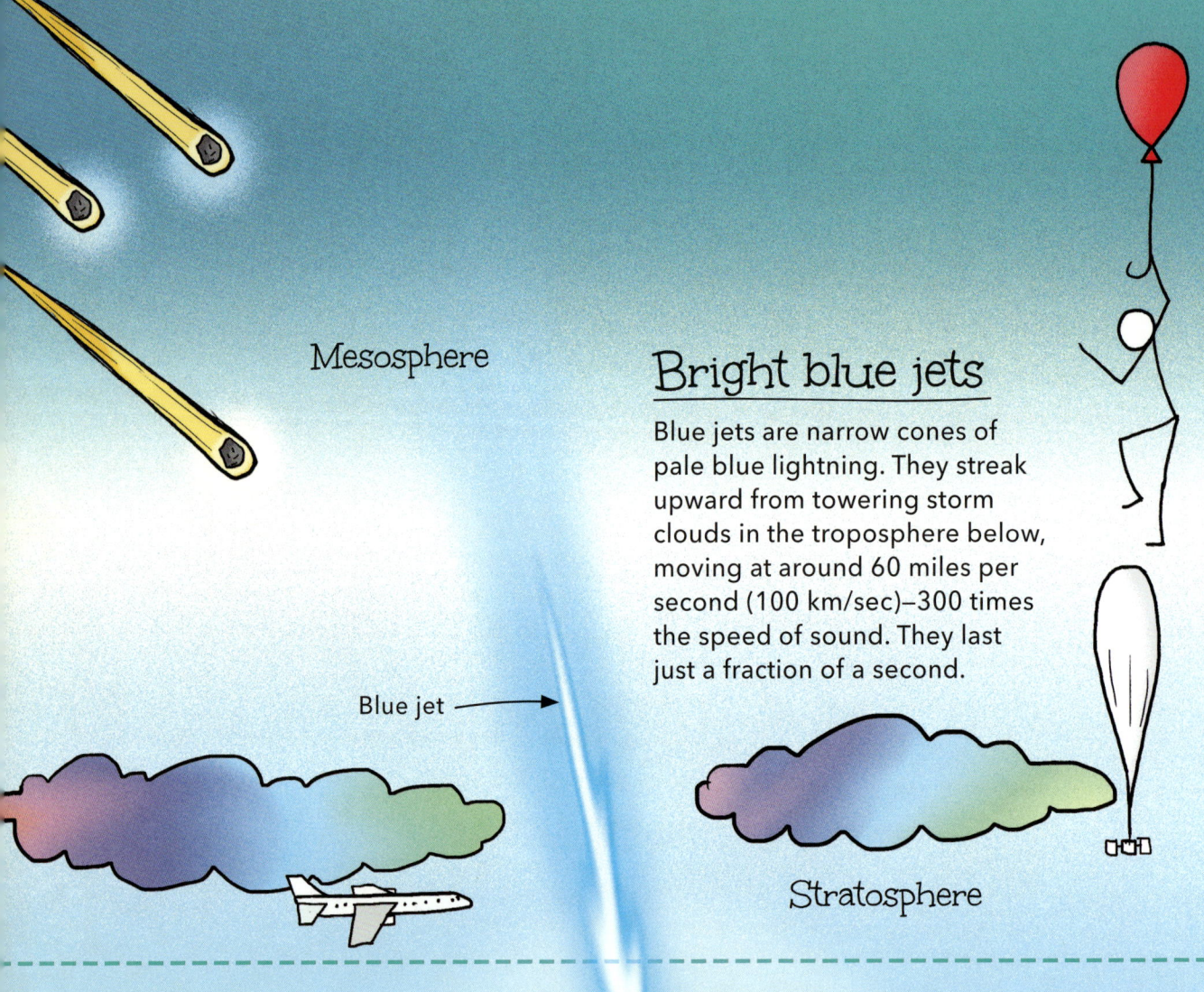

Mesosphere

Bright blue jets

Blue jets are narrow cones of pale blue lightning. They streak upward from towering storm clouds in the troposphere below, moving at around 60 miles per second (100 km/sec)—300 times the speed of sound. They last just a fraction of a second.

Blue jet

Stratosphere

Troposphere

Storm cloud

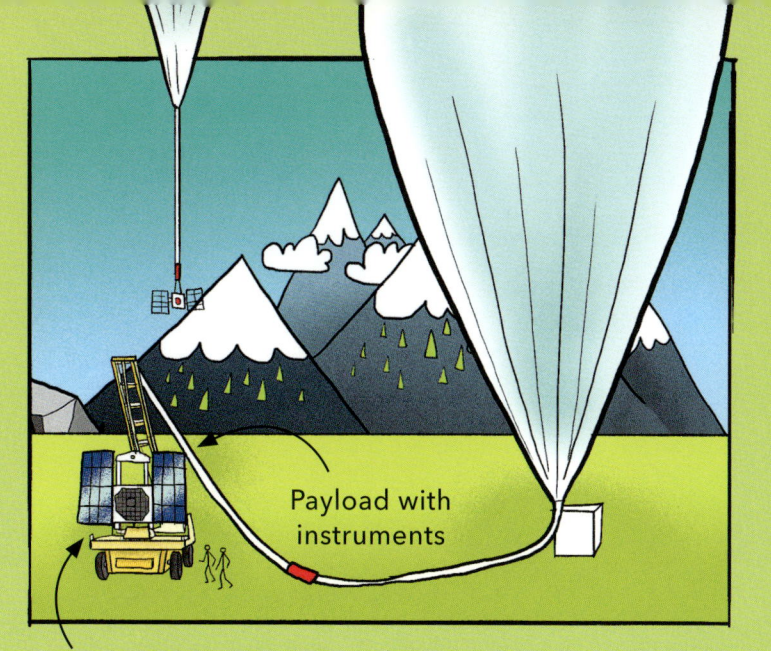

Studying weather

Every day, hundreds of huge weather balloons, 6 feet (1.8 m) in diameter, rise 20 miles (32 km) into the stratosphere. Each carries a radiosonde, which is a small bundle of instruments. These transmit data, such as temperature, pressure, wind speeds, and heat radiation levels, to scientists, helping them to understand more about weather and climate.

Payload with instruments

Transporter

Jetting high

Jet aircraft fly as much as possible in the lower part of the stratosphere, which is more stable than the stormy troposphere beneath it. The temperature in the stratosphere rises steadily and evenly with height, so hot and cold air mix less and there is less turbulence. Here, jet stream winds help pilots to fly faster and save fuel.

Stable jet stream

Warm, moist air

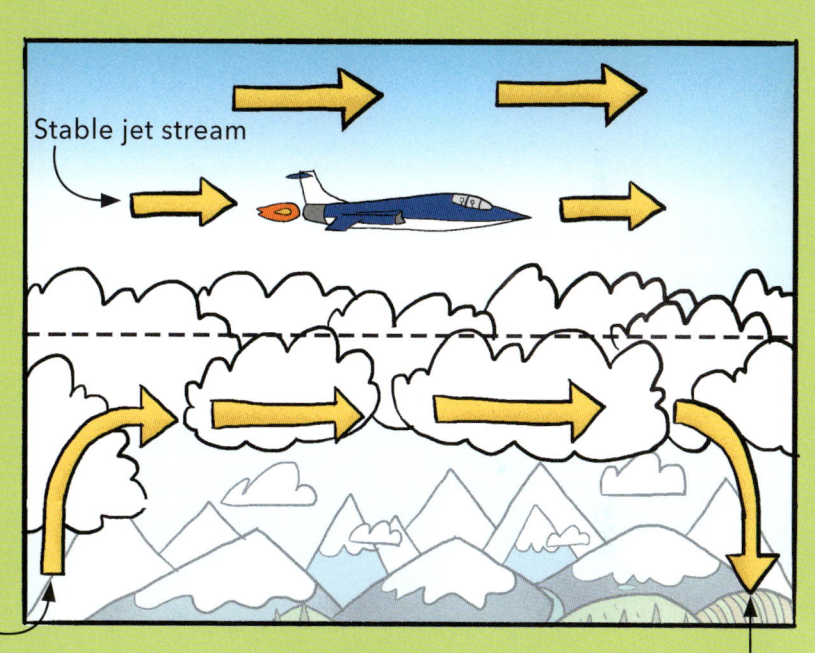

Rain or snow

Bright nacreous cloud

Wavy clouds

Mother-of-pearl, or "nacreous," clouds in the stratosphere light up the evening sky with waves of rainbow colors, mostly at or toward the poles. They can be caused by winds much lower down and occur at heights of around 13 miles (20 km). They are also known as winter polar stratospheric clouds (PSCs).

19

The Ozone Layer

The protective ozone layer lies within the stratosphere around 10 to 24 miles (16-38 km) above Earth. Ozone is a type of oxygen molecule that can absorb the most harmful, burning UV light from the sun, which prevents most of it from reaching the ground.

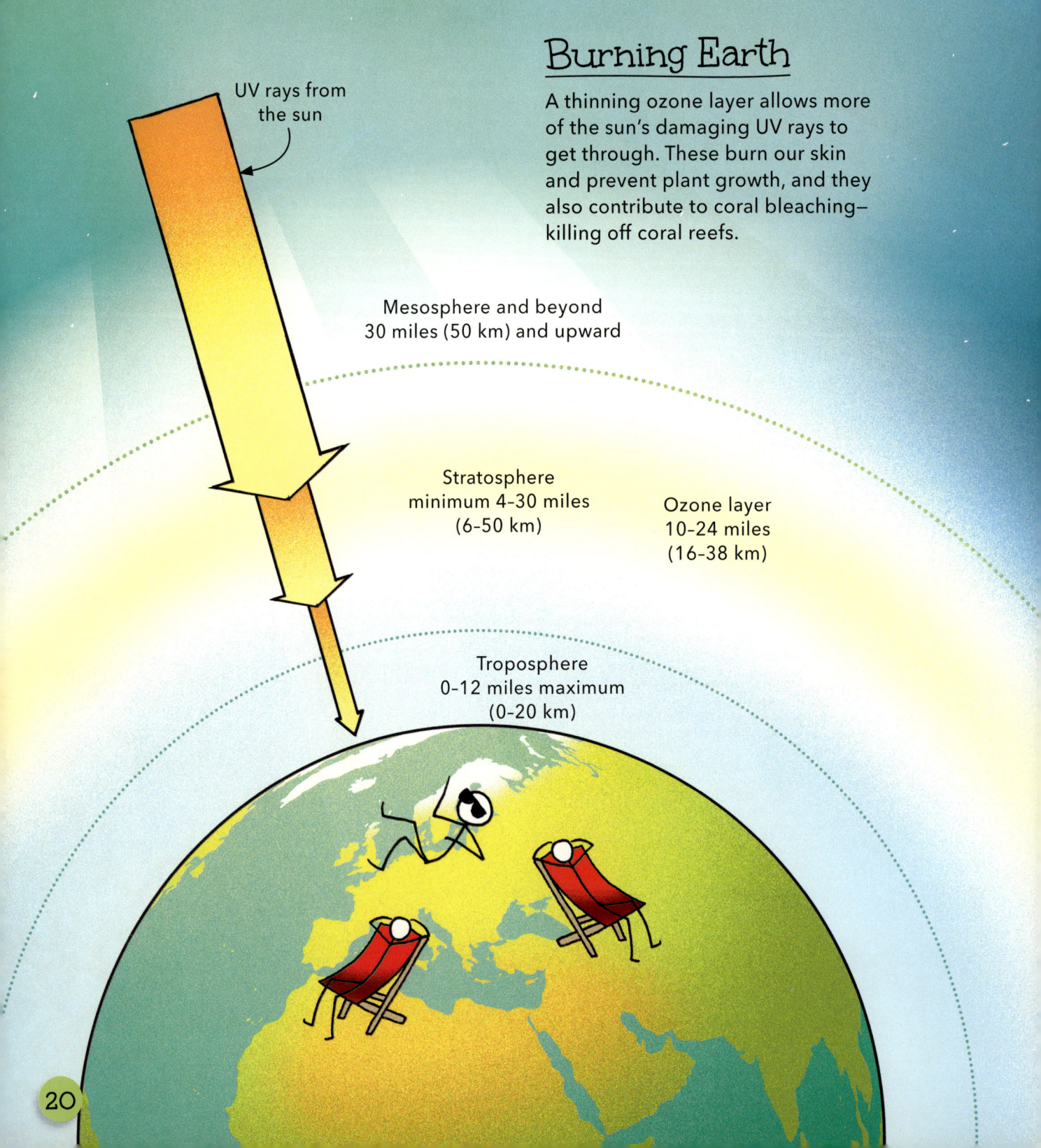

Burning Earth

A thinning ozone layer allows more of the sun's damaging UV rays to get through. These burn our skin and prevent plant growth, and they also contribute to coral bleaching—killing off coral reefs.

UV rays from the sun

Mesosphere and beyond
30 miles (50 km) and upward

Stratosphere
minimum 4-30 miles
(6-50 km)

Ozone layer
10-24 miles
(16-38 km)

Troposphere
0-12 miles maximum
(0-20 km)

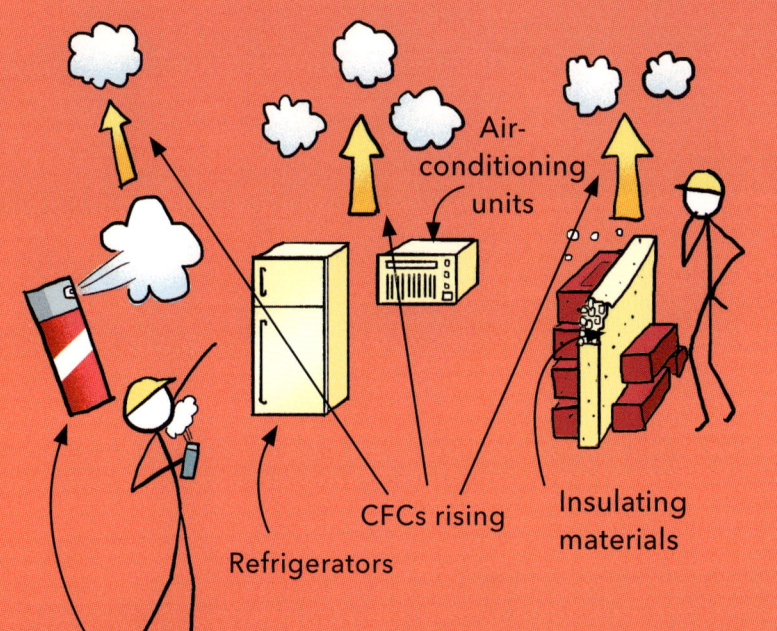

Damaging gases

In the 1980s, it was found that, when gases called cholorfluorocarbons (CFCs) were exposed to the sun's strong UV light, they released chlorine into the atmosphere. This caused the ozone layer to become thinner. So CFCs, which were used in aerosols, air-conditioning units, refrigerators, and insulating materials, were banned.

Air-conditioning units

CFCs rising

Insulating materials

Refrigerators

Aerosols

Thinning ozone layer

Thinning layer

The "hole" in the ozone layer is actually a region where the layer is thinner, especially over the poles in springtime. It was discovered in the Antarctic in 1984 by the British scientist Joseph Farman, who used a ground-level instrument called the Dobson spectrophotometer, or Dobsonmeter. Now, thermal images from space satellites track the size and shape of the hole.

Dobsonmeter

Measuring the ozone layer

A Dobsonmeter works out how much ozone there is absorbing the sun's UV rays in the atmosphere. It was invented by the British meteorologist Gordon Dobson in the 1920s. Ozone levels in Antarctica reduced by about 50 percent in the worst years.

Earth's Troposphere

The troposphere is the layer that wraps immediately around Earth's surface. It reaches from 0 mile, or sea level, up to variable heights of 4 to 12 miles (6–20 km). It is the warmest layer, because Earth absorbs the sun's warmth, then radiates it back up, heating the air near the ground.

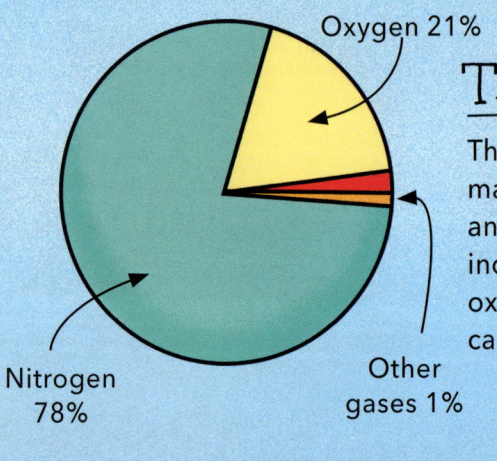

Oxygen 21%
Nitrogen 78%
Other gases 1%

The air we breathe

The troposphere is made up of mainly nitrogen with some oxygen and small amounts of other gases, including carbon dioxide. We need oxygen to breathe, and plants use carbon dioxide to grow.

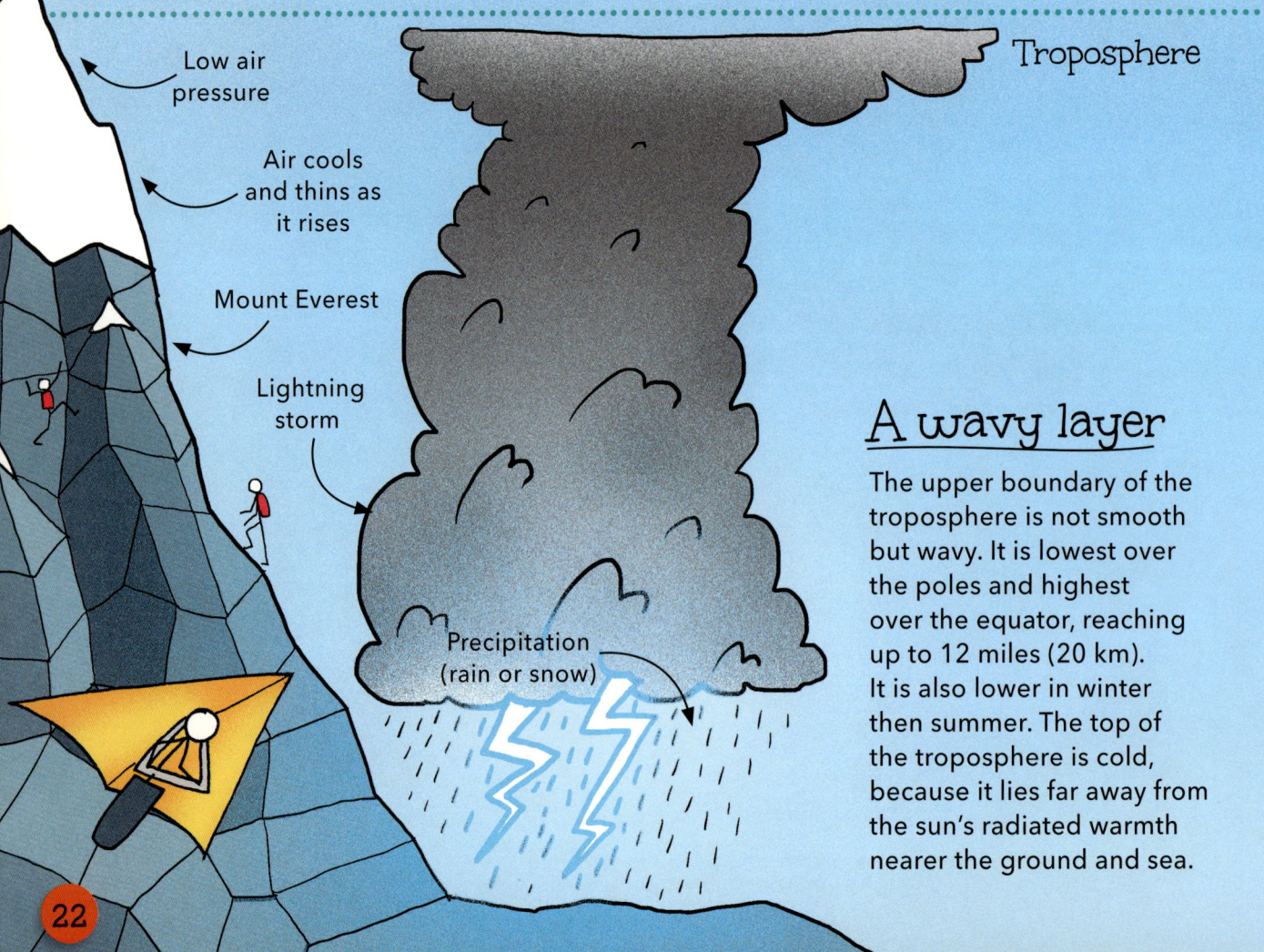

Troposphere

Low air pressure
Air cools and thins as it rises
Mount Everest
Lightning storm
Precipitation (rain or snow)

A wavy layer

The upper boundary of the troposphere is not smooth but wavy. It is lowest over the poles and highest over the equator, reaching up to 12 miles (20 km). It is also lower in winter then summer. The top of the troposphere is cold, because it lies far away from the sun's radiated warmth nearer the ground and sea.

Thinner on top

Air gets thinner toward the top of the troposphere as air pressure drops. So there is less oxygen, which is why mountaineers usually carry oxygen supplies. This is also why airplane cabins are pressurized, providing the right oxygen levels and pressure for passengers and crew to breathe. Despite this, Rüppell's griffon vulture, one of the highest flying birds, has been recorded in flight at 36,000 feet (10,900 m)—even higher than an average commercial airliner.

Earth's water cycle

High in the troposphere, tall cloud columns rise. These form when the sun heats up water from oceans and large lakes. The water evaporates from a liquid to a gas, which rises as it warms. High up, it cools and condenses into water droplets that form clouds. When the droplets are heavy enough, they fall as rain.

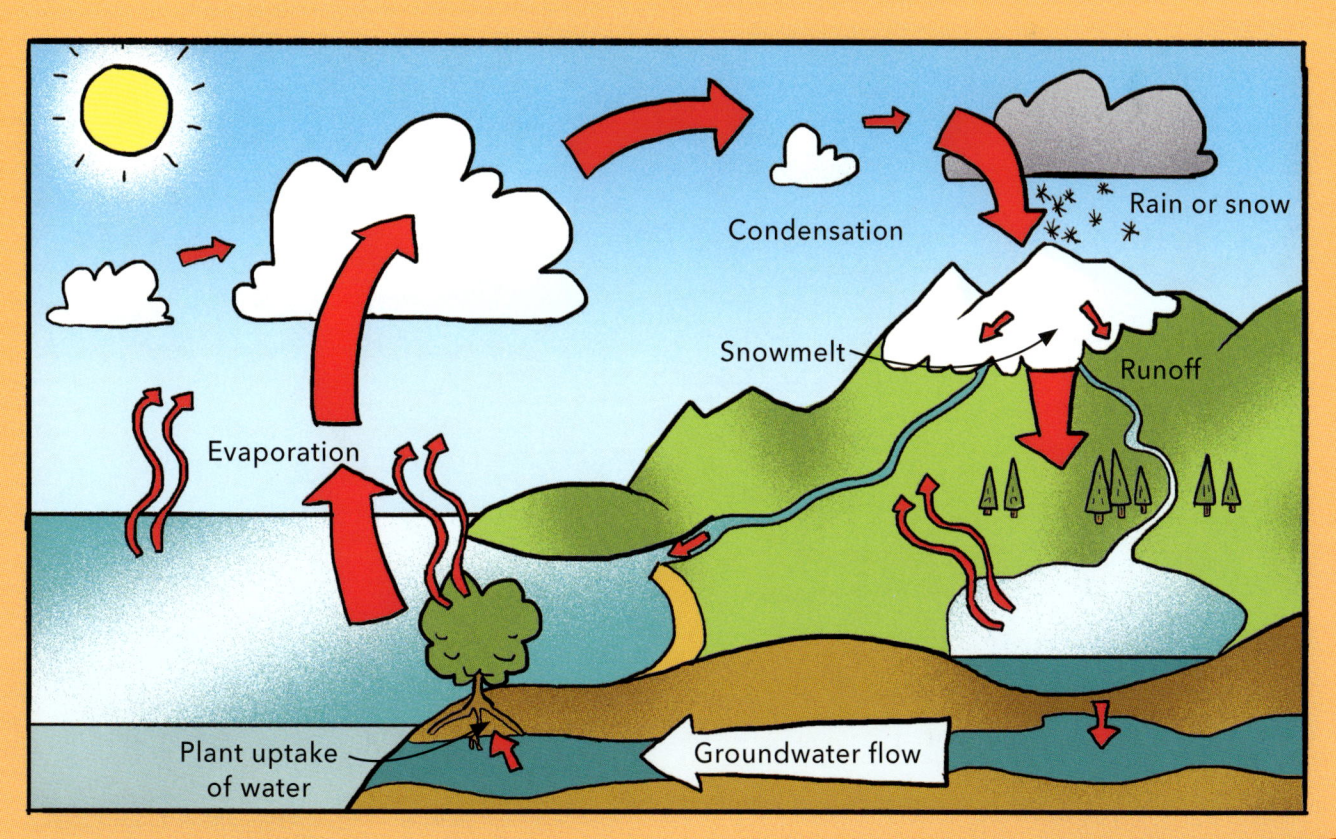

Storms and Twisters

Towering clouds in the troposphere bring strong winds, pouring rain, and snow blizzards. The most destructive storms are called hurricanes, cyclones, or typhoons, depending on where they blow. Twisting tornadoes suck up all that lies in their path.

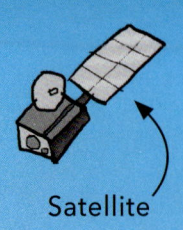

Satellite

Hurricane in action

Storm motion

Clear, cloudless eye of storm

Weather balloon

Cold air

Warm, moist air

Warm updraft (upward air current)

Cold downdraft (downward air current)

Radar

Rain

Hurricanes from space

Satellites track the paths of hurricanes, which are wide banks of storm clouds rotating around a calm center (called the "eye"). Hurricanes develop over warm oceans, where winds pick up huge amounts of moist air. The moisture rises and forms clouds that are swirled around by driving winds. Hurricanes smack the land with destructive force and push up enormous waves, causing serious flooding.

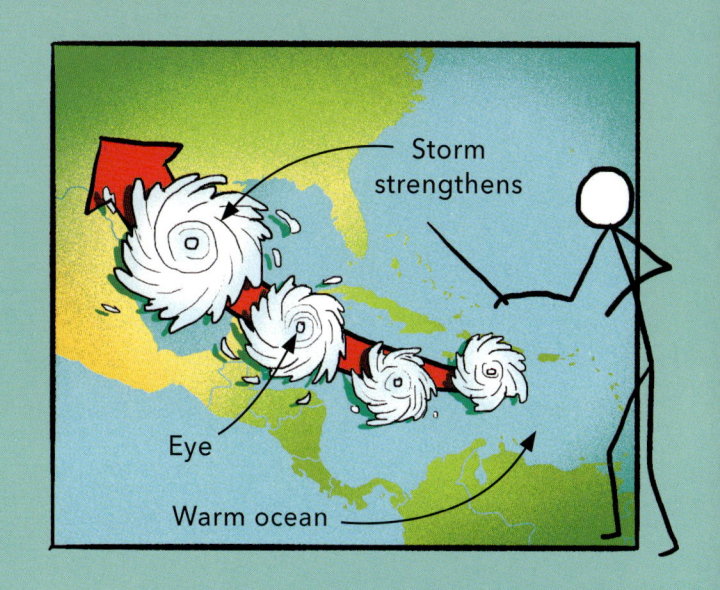

Storm strengthens
Eye
Warm ocean

Making rain

Climate change is making some regions on Earth drier. In some dry zones, rain clouds are artificially created. This is done by "seeding" the air with chemicals. They draw together any water droplets in the air to form clouds. The chemicals can be spread by aircraft or released by rockets and other launching equipment from the ground.

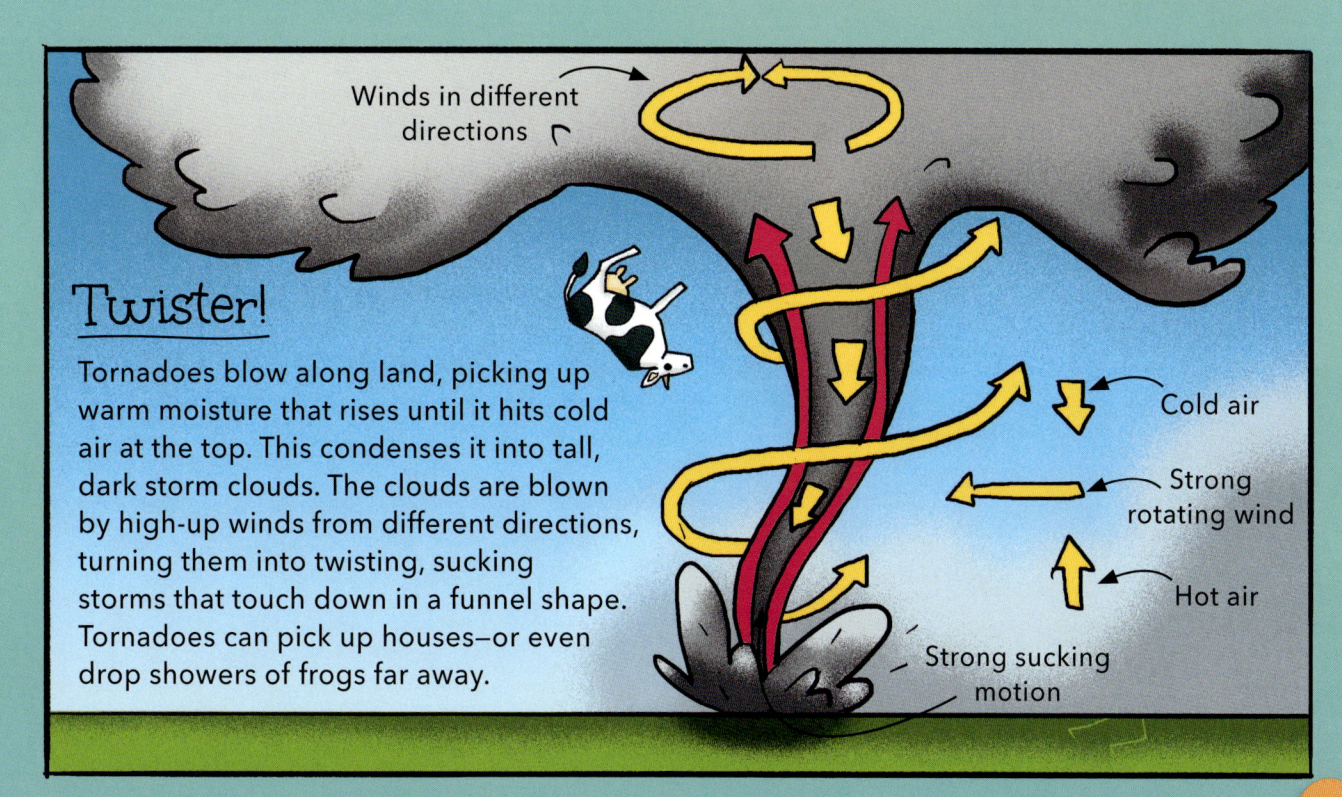

Seed-clouding machine

Twister!

Tornadoes blow along land, picking up warm moisture that rises until it hits cold air at the top. This condenses it into tall, dark storm clouds. The clouds are blown by high-up winds from different directions, turning them into twisting, sucking storms that touch down in a funnel shape. Tornadoes can pick up houses—or even drop showers of frogs far away.

Winds in different directions
Cold air
Strong rotating wind
Hot air
Strong sucking motion

What's the Weather Like?

Weather encompasses the heat, cold, rain, snow, fog, and wind that affect us every day on Earth. Observers at weather stations monitor temperature, humidity, wind speed and direction, and rain or snow fall on a daily and hourly basis. Their data is vital for making weather forecasts for people's safety and to study climate change.

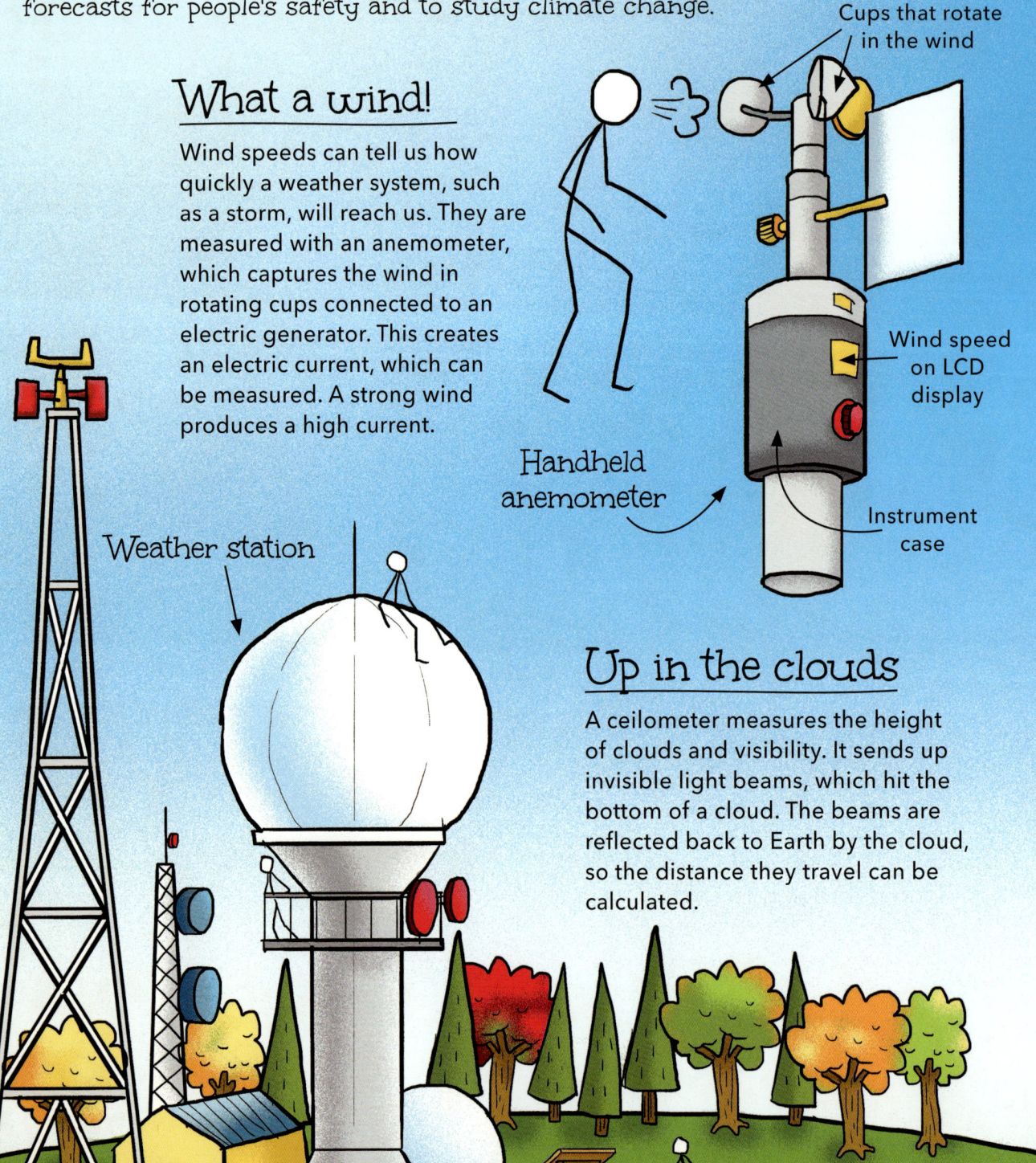

What a wind!

Wind speeds can tell us how quickly a weather system, such as a storm, will reach us. They are measured with an anemometer, which captures the wind in rotating cups connected to an electric generator. This creates an electric current, which can be measured. A strong wind produces a high current.

Cups that rotate in the wind

Wind speed on LCD display

Instrument case

Handheld anemometer

Weather station

Up in the clouds

A ceilometer measures the height of clouds and visibility. It sends up invisible light beams, which hit the bottom of a cloud. The beams are reflected back to Earth by the cloud, so the distance they travel can be calculated.

Ceilometer

How hot is it?

The first true thermometer for measuring temperature accurately was invented in 1724 by German physicist Gabriel Fahrenheit. He set a column of mercury, enclosed in glass, against a scale of measurement. Alcohol is now used instead of mercury, which is dangerous. Digital thermometers (right) are the latest technology, as well as safe. These can have a wireless sensor to use at a distance from the main unit. We still use degrees Fahrenheit as a temperature scale.

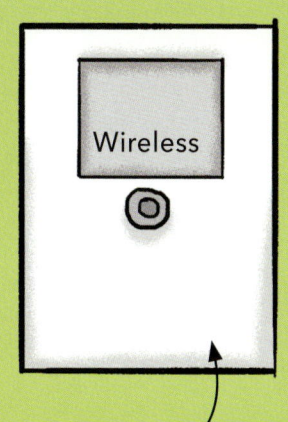

Indoor 64.9 °F
Outdoor 75.2 °F
8:04

Digital thermometer

Wireless

Wireless sensor for relaying temperature data to the receiver unit

Under pressure

Air pressure is the pressure exerted by the weight of air pushing down on Earth from above. It tells us roughly the type of weather we can expect for a few days. High air pressure usually brings clear skies and sunshine; low air pressure means rain, or a storm. Barometers measure air pressure.

Barometer

Hygrometer

Measuring humidity

We use a hygrometer to measure the air's moisture, or humidity. It tells us how much water vapor is in the air and when it will form water droplets. This is important in such processes as applying paint coatings, as well as in conserving artworks and musical instruments.

Mountains and Valleys

Earth, the sun, and other planets in our solar system formed nearly 4.6 billion years ago. Gases and dust in space collided, merging into clumps that enlarged as their gravity attracted more material. On the clump that became Earth, a cooling crust cracked into huge pieces called tectonic plates, which covered hotter layers and a hardening core.

Mountaintops
Where winters are cold, snow and ice reach far down the mountains. In warm parts of the world, snow and ice give way to alpine trees and plants.

Plains
Down on the plains, vast grasslands stretch out in both cool and hot climates. Here, wild animals roam and farmers herd cattle and grow cereals.

Under the Crust
Below the plains, rivers cut deep down into the rock. Even deeper, Earth shakes and hot volcanic magma pushes up through the crust.

Earth's Core
At the center of Earth, a soft, searing-hot outer core wraps around the hard inner core. Both parts of the core are made mostly of metal.

29

Snow power

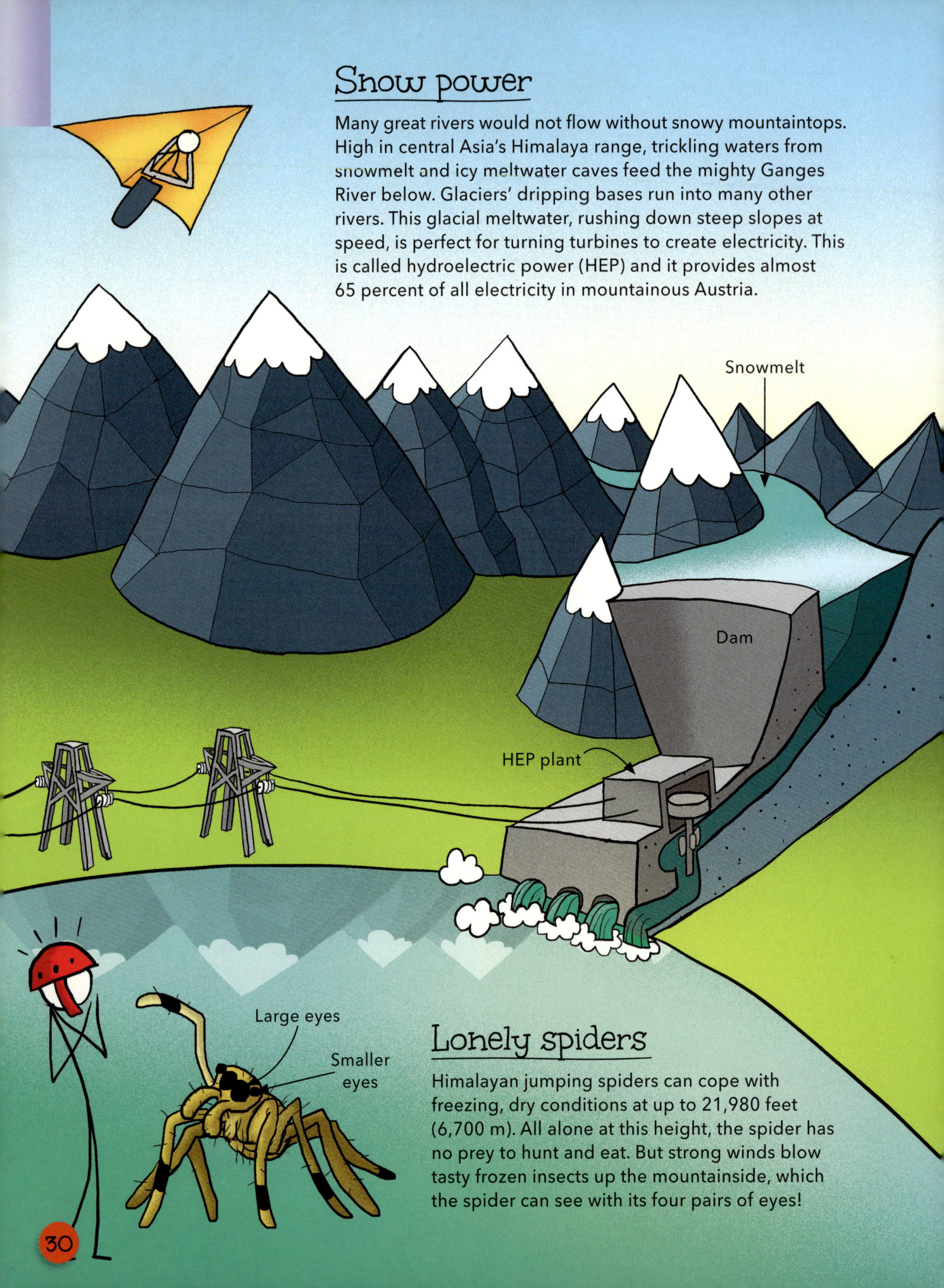

Many great rivers would not flow without snowy mountaintops. High in central Asia's Himalaya range, trickling waters from snowmelt and icy meltwater caves feed the mighty Ganges River below. Glaciers' dripping bases run into many other rivers. This glacial meltwater, rushing down steep slopes at speed, is perfect for turning turbines to create electricity. This is called hydroelectric power (HEP) and it provides almost 65 percent of all electricity in mountainous Austria.

Snowmelt

Dam

HEP plant

Large eyes

Smaller eyes

Lonely spiders

Himalayan jumping spiders can cope with freezing, dry conditions at up to 21,980 feet (6,700 m). All alone at this height, the spider has no prey to hunt and eat. But strong winds blow tasty frozen insects up the mountainside, which the spider can see with its four pairs of eyes!

Snowy Peaks

We live on the top crusty layer of Earth—the solid, brittle lithosphere. Here, the hardest rocks wear down more slowly than the softer rocks, leaving high, windy mountain peaks coated with snow and thick ice.

Challenge at the top

Mount Everest is the world's highest peak above sea level, rising to 29,035 feet (8,850 m). It's a magnet for serious mountaineers. In freezing conditions, they have spiked crampons on their shoes to grip the ice and an ice pick to pull themselves up.

Helmet

Carabiner (safety rope hook)

Ice pick

Crampons

Ridge

Glacier (ice tongue)

Clinging on

Clusters of spongy, plantlike lichens cling to the rocks on the lowest, warmer parts of this layer. Lichens are combinations of fungi and algae.

Tough Alpine Life

Down the mountain, the treeline marks the alpine layer. Here, the trees' waxy, needlelike leaves stop them from freezing or drying out in winter. Creatures, such as small shrews, hibernate in winter, their heart rate slowing down so they use little energy.

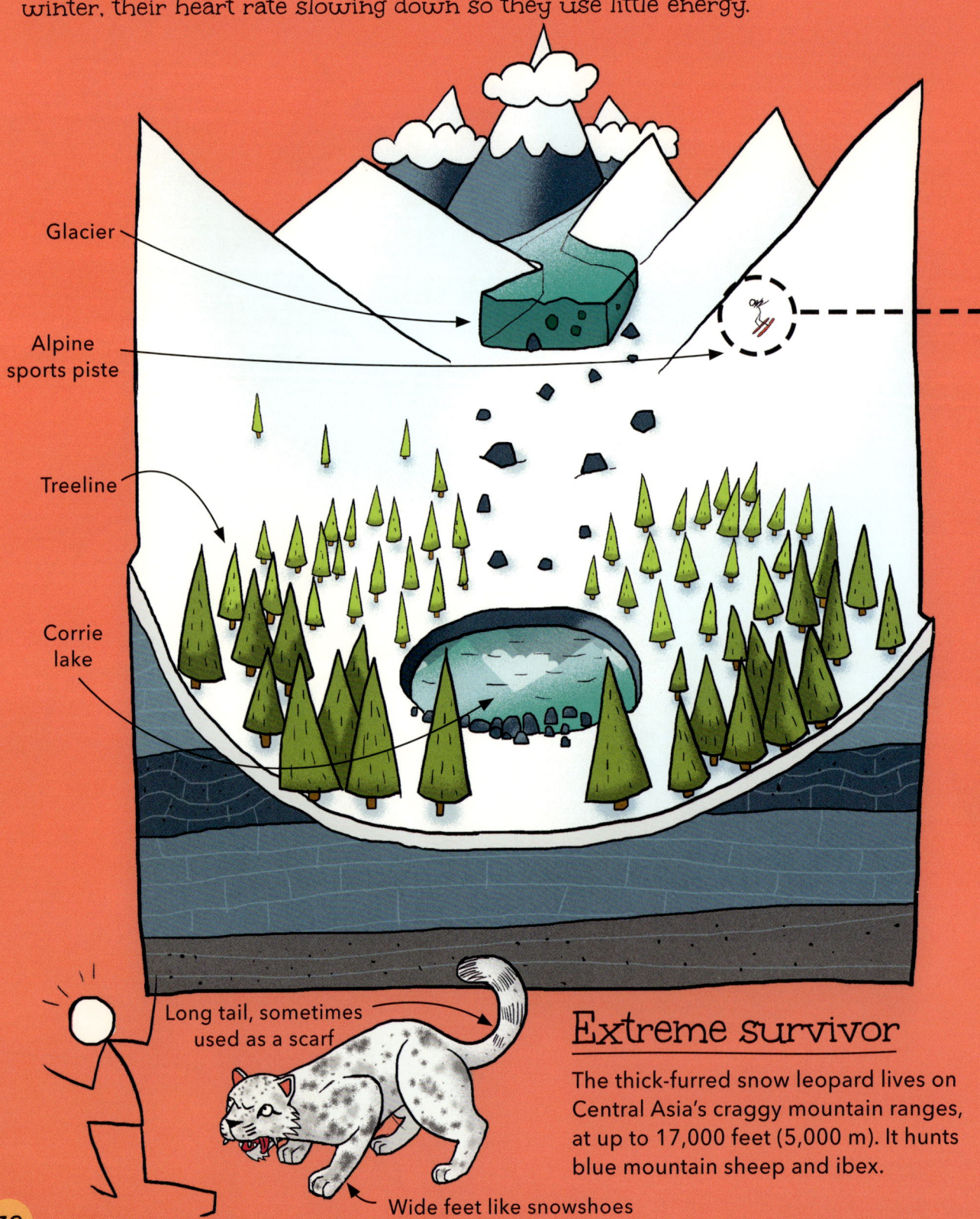

- Glacier
- Alpine sports piste
- Treeline
- Corrie lake

Long tail, sometimes used as a scarf

Wide feet like snowshoes

Extreme survivor

The thick-furred snow leopard lives on Central Asia's craggy mountain ranges, at up to 17,000 feet (5,000 m). It hunts blue mountain sheep and ibex.

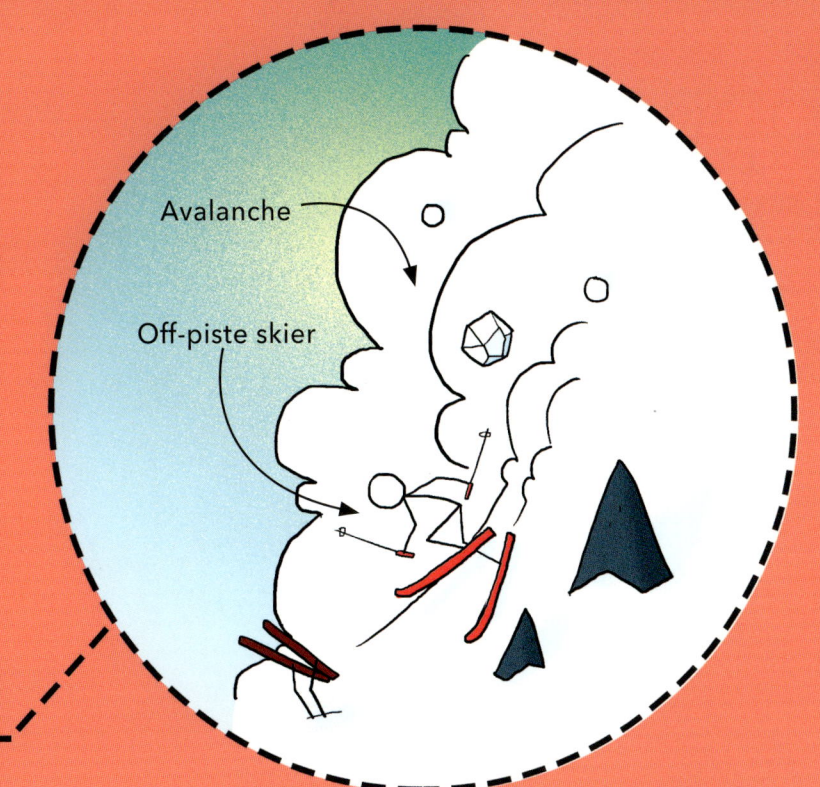

Spectacular sports

In the United States alone, nearly ten million people a year ski or snowboard. Most glide down pistes, which are runs of specially prepared, hard-packed snow. But more daring, off-piste sports take place in higher backcountry. Here, skiers powder ski fast between trees on loose, unstable snow. Cat skiers, named after the snowcats that transport them, descend down deep, steep trails. Splitboarders climb high on skis, then clip the skis together to board their way down again. These thrill seekers carry GPS devices to beam their position if avalanches of snow bury them.

Avalanche
Off-piste skier

Icy lakes

Rounded lakes called corries form on mountainsides. They begin in small hollows, where snow layers pack down hard and ice is created. Gravity pulls the ice downward in a circular motion, abrading—or scouring out—a bigger hole that fills with water. Many corrie lakes formed thousands of years ago.

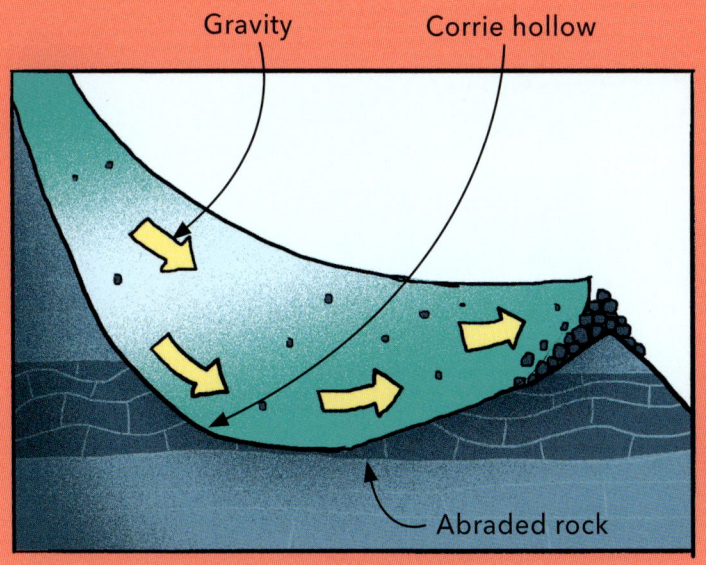

Gravity
Corrie hollow
Abraded rock

Brave flowers

Low-growing, cushion-shaped plants hug the rocks to resist high alpine winds. Many have long taproots to anchor them. Their tightly packed flowers bloom quickly in the short summers, which last three months or so. Dark leaves absorb the sunlight they use to make the plant's food.

Alpine *Diapensia* plant
Tight, low mound
Dark leaves

Forested Slopes

Lower, gentler mountain slopes are known as the montane layer, and they have thicker soil where vast forests of trees, bushes, and grasses grow. Close to the hot equator, tropical and subtropical trees flourish. Near the chilly poles, hardy evergreen spruces and pines survive.

Cool coffee

Coffee grown on bushes high up has the best flavor. Wild coffee comes from the mountains of Ethiopia in East Africa and has been cultivated for more than 600 years.

Red coffee berries

Coffee bean inside

Montain slopes

Coffee farm

Orchard

Widening river

Pine and spruce trees

34

Bright birds

Subtropical montane forest birds are often brightly colored to attract a mate among the trees' shadows. The vivid green-tailed sunbird occupies a broad range, from the forests of western Nepal and northern India down into Southeast Asia. The Golden-browed chlorophonia lives in the canopy of the highland forests of southern Central America.

Green-tailed sunbird

Golden-browed chlorophonia

Juniper and conifer forest

Montane apple orchard

Montane mammals

Both hot and cold montane climates are rich habitats for mammals, both large and small. In North America, the black bear climbs forest trees to reach berries and fruit, but it also eats roots, fish, and insects. The black bear comes in a variety of colors, but they all have thick fur to help them through winter hibernation. In eastern Africa, furry mountain gorillas live in high cloud forests. They feed on forest fruit, bamboo shoots, thistles, and dried grasses.

Sedges

Skeleton trees

These dried-out, bent spruce or pine trees are called *krummholz*, which means "twisted wood." Krummholz are stunted by extreme winter cold and blown in one direction by severe freezing winds. As they bend, branches touch the ground. Roots can grow down from these branches, anchoring the tree firmly.

Wind direction ⟶

On the Plains

Vast grasslands spread out beneath mountain foothills, sometimes on raised plateaus. North America's prairies, South America's pampas, Central Asia's cool steppes, and Africa's hot savanna have provided highways for migrating peoples and creatures.

Riches beneath

Mining and oil and gas extraction break up the grasslands' wild beauty. It is easier to transport minerals and energy sources on the flat plains than in hilly terrain.

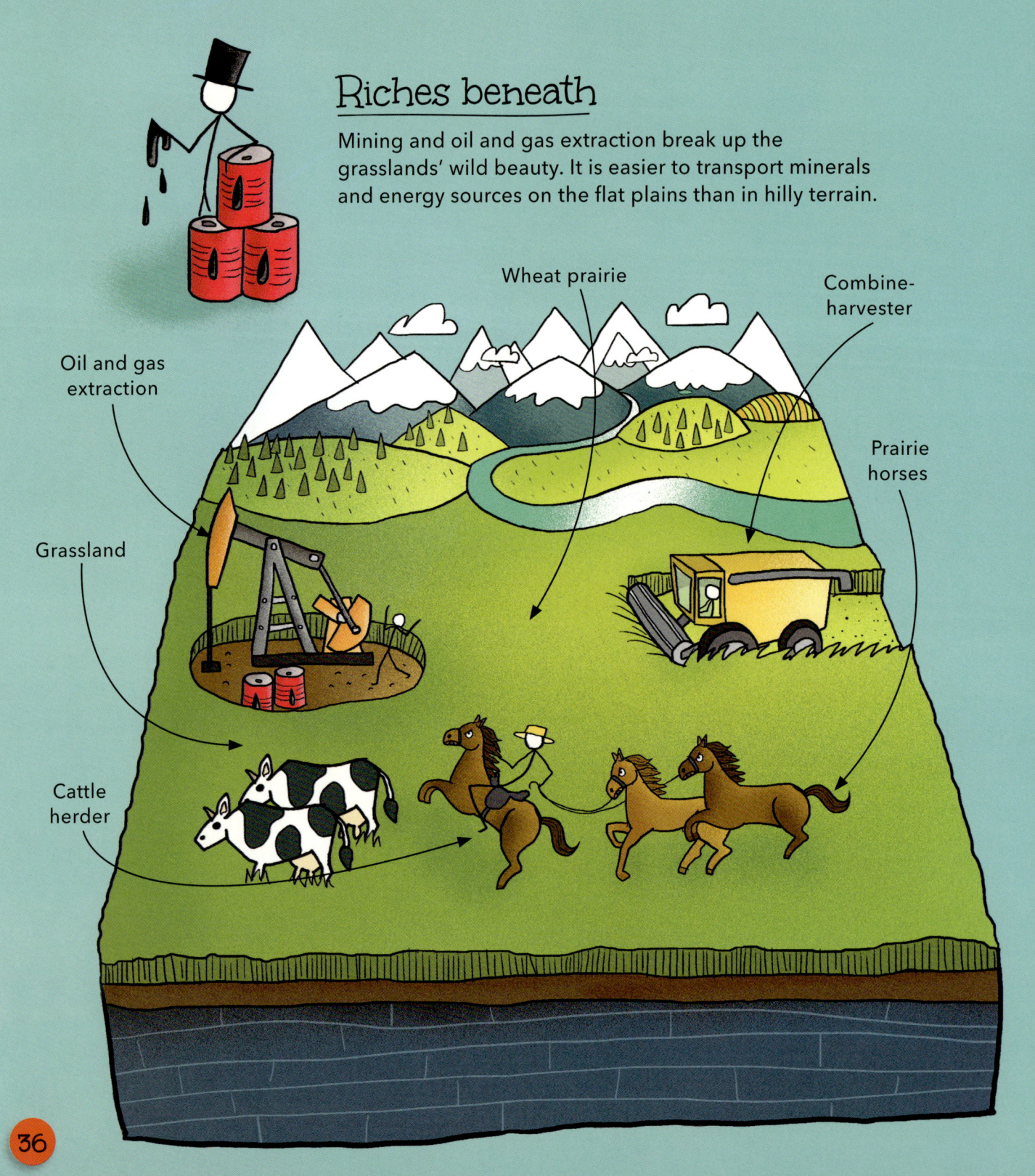

Wheat prairie

Combine-harvester

Oil and gas extraction

Prairie horses

Grassland

Cattle herder

Farming on the plains

Many grasslands have been cleared to cultivate grass species, such as wheat and corn. In Africa, these are planted together with beans, which help fertilize the soil. Argentina has recently converted some pampas to huge vineyards, although cattle are still herded on these vast grasslands.

Wheat field

Attwater's prairie chicken

Hiding in the grass

Carpets of grasses and flowers are perfect camouflage for small mammals and birds. The mottled brown Attwater's prairie chicken hides among Texas coast prairie bluestem and switchgrass plants. But the adult male Attwater's appears in shorter grasses to call for a mate, his loud boom reaching 2,600 feet (800 m).

Prairie grasses and flowers

Teeming with life

Grassland plains are teeming with wildlife. Africa's savanna creatures range from tiny termites to huge elephants, Earth's largest land animal. Termites build earth mounds that can reach 17 feet (5 m). The termites' constant burrowing helps to circulate nutrients, keeping the soil healthy. Large grassland mammals, such as buffalo and antelope, fertilize the soil with their droppings, which contain seeds that get scattered across the vast grassland plains.

Termite mound

The Valley Floor

Glaciers carve broad valleys down through mountains. Rivers cut deep natural highways into the lowlands, widening as they reach the sea. Manmade transport systems take advantage of the shallow slopes far along a river's course.

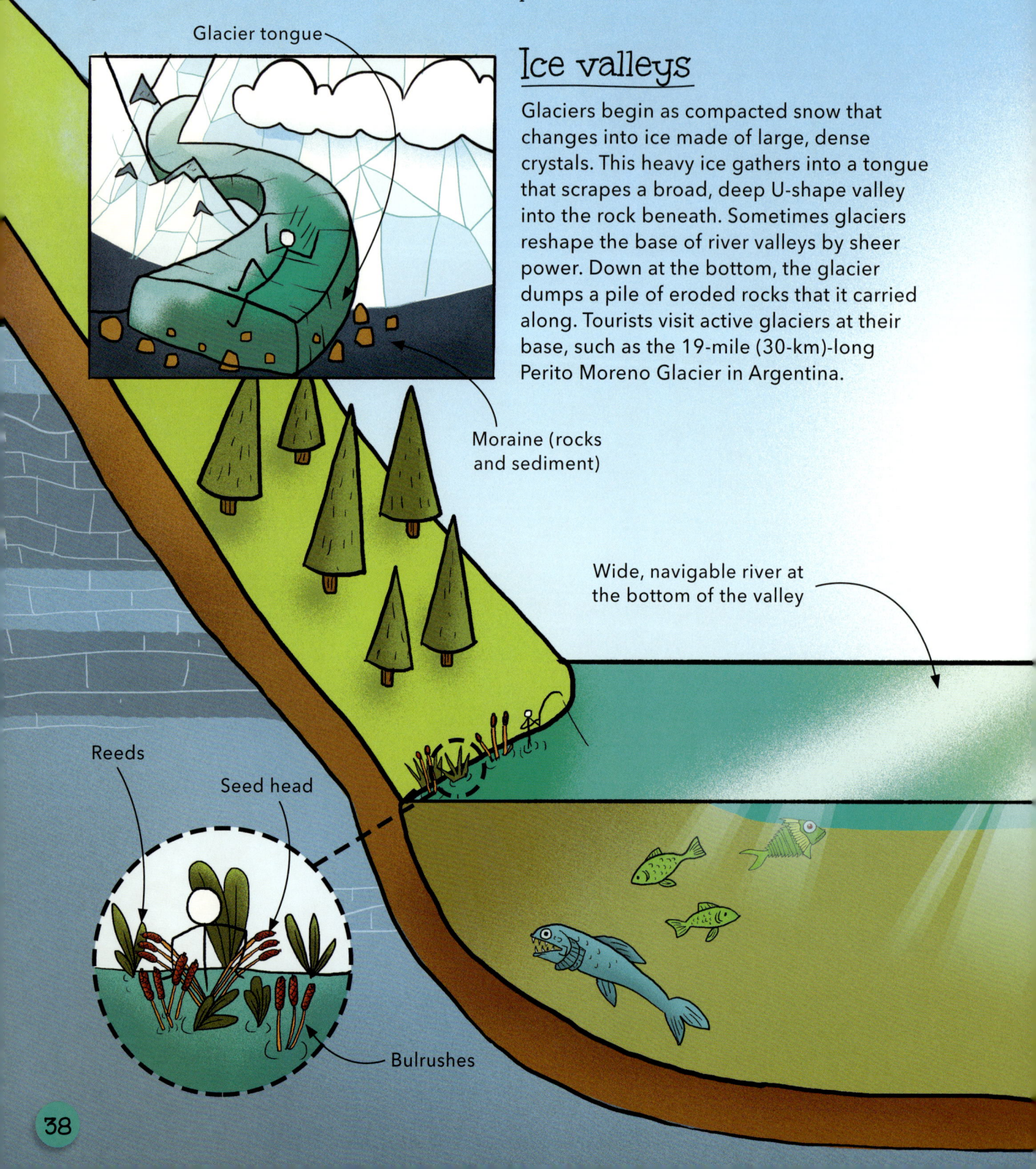

Glacier tongue

Ice valleys

Glaciers begin as compacted snow that changes into ice made of large, dense crystals. This heavy ice gathers into a tongue that scrapes a broad, deep U-shape valley into the rock beneath. Sometimes glaciers reshape the base of river valleys by sheer power. Down at the bottom, the glacier dumps a pile of eroded rocks that it carried along. Tourists visit active glaciers at their base, such as the 19-mile (30-km)-long Perito Moreno Glacier in Argentina.

Moraine (rocks and sediment)

Wide, navigable river at the bottom of the valley

Reeds

Seed head

Bulrushes

River power

Rivers carve steep, narrow, V-shape valleys until they reach low, flat land. Here, they weaken, widen, and wind, no longer able to cut downward. Meeting the sea, rivers may split into tiny rivulets, spreading out into a delta. India's Ganges River has the world's largest delta—it is 38,610 square miles (100,000 km^2).

Big fish

Wide rivers teem with large, tasty fish. One of these is the salmon, which lays its eggs in river gravel beds in fall. In spring, the fish hatch. After a few years in the river, they swim far out to sea. Here, they feed on sand eels and herring until they return to the river once again.

Ship for transporting goods

Railtrack along level river valley bottom

Rushes and reeds

Grasslike reeds and rushes grow near the banks of a river, low down on its course. Bulrushes are habitats for fish and amphibians, such as frogs and newts. The bulrush's leaves and spikes are edible.

Reed habitat for fish and amphibians

39

Deep in the Canyon

Canyons are plunging, steep valleys. Some are cut by thin rivers, while others are splits caused by the movement of tectonic plates deep in Earth's crust. The deepest canyon, at 17,490 feet (5,300 m), is Tibet's Yarlung Zangbo Canyon.

Ancient canyon dwellers

Many prehistoric humans lived in canyon caves. They used rock pigments to depict their lives on the walls. East Africa's Olduvai Gorge holds some of the oldest fossilized human remains.

Ancient rock art

Rock layers

River, restricted by canyon sides

Buzzing with birds

Canyons are remote havens for some of the world's rarest birds. Great eagles, condors, and falcons circle up above, their sharp eyes focusing on prey far below. High, dry ledges are perfect for their nests. Lower down, small, bright perching birds, such as warblers, flycatchers, and orioles, thrive in the damp habitat.

Bald eagle

Bubbling waters

Hot volcanic activity lies close to the surface of some canyon floors. Here, hot magma below heats groundwater above, thrusting it up into hot waterspouts, or geysers. Boiling springs, bubbling mud pools, and steaming sprays of water are dotted across the landscapes in these canyons. California's Yellowstone Park holds about 500 hot springs and geysers. Across the world in Africa's Great Rift Valley, Kenya is using volcanic steam wells to harness geothermal energy.

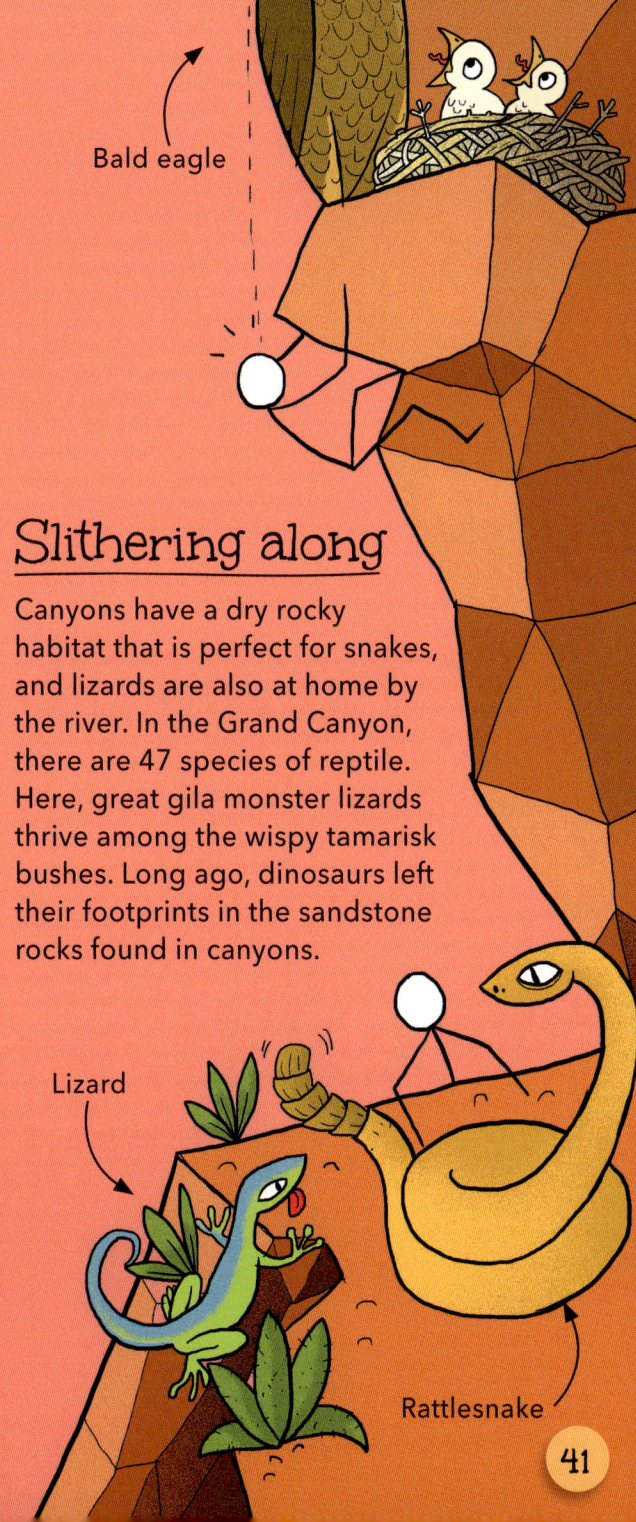

Hot spring Spouting geyser Steam vent

Heated groundwater Volcanic magma

Slithering along

Canyons have a dry rocky habitat that is perfect for snakes, and lizards are also at home by the river. In the Grand Canyon, there are 47 species of reptile. Here, great gila monster lizards thrive among the wispy tamarisk bushes. Long ago, dinosaurs left their footprints in the sandstone rocks found in canyons.

Lizard

Rattlesnake

Down the Mine

Deep into Earth's crust, humans drill down for precious minerals and metals embedded in rock. Most hard minerals are formed from hot volcanic magma. Slow cooling and high pressure caused some magma particles to crystallize into sparkling stones.

Precious metals

Gold is a metallic element that can be found in river deposits. However, gold is mostly embedded in veins of quartz rock, deep below Earth's surface.

Gold deposit

Coal or ore transported to the surface for processing

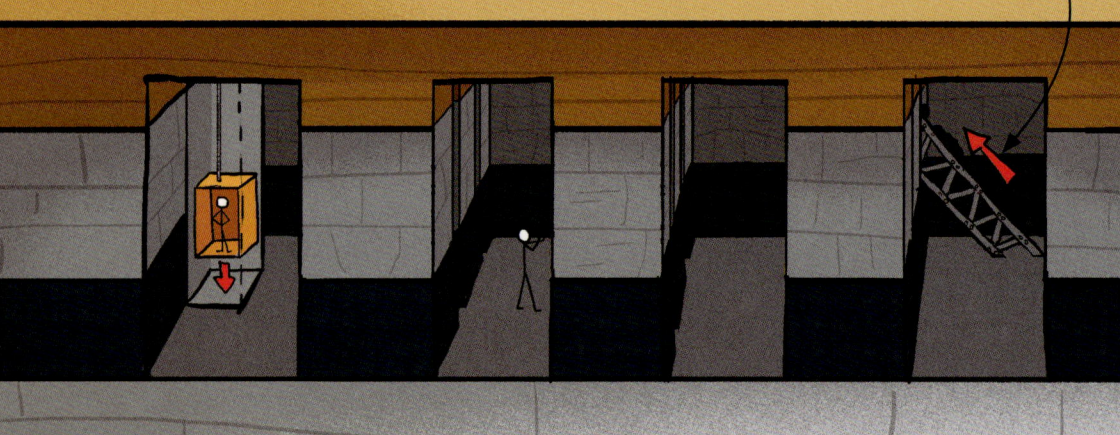

42

Brilliant diamonds

Diamond mines create terraced craters so large that they can be seen from space. Diamonds are hard, heat-resistant carbons. They began to form about 4,600 million years ago in Earth's hot mantle, but were thrust up by deep volcanic eruptions. Russia has more than half the world's largest diamond mines.

Diamond mine terraces

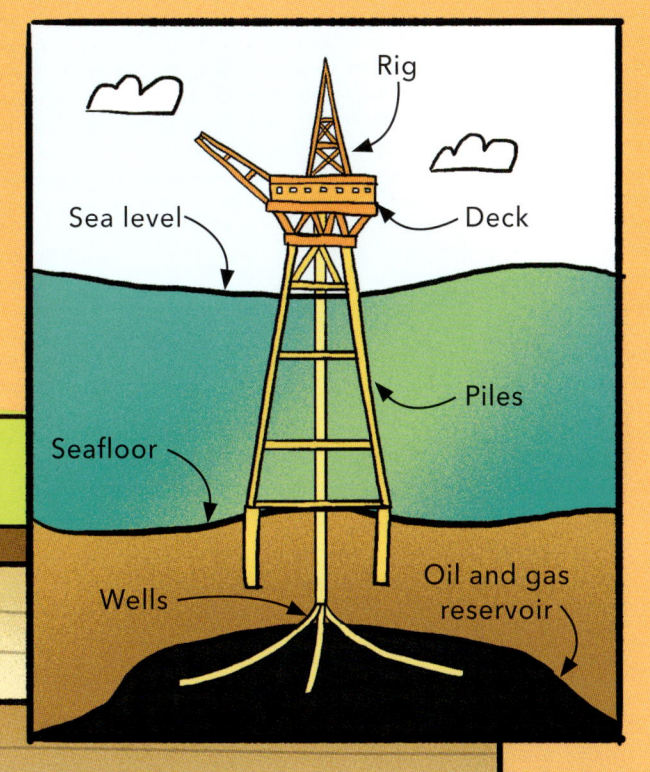

Crushed creatures

We dig deeper for oil and gas deposits than for any other mineral. The deepest floating oil platform is Perdido, in the Gulf of Mexico. Its pipe reaches down 8,000 feet (2,450 m). Drills access pockets of fossil fuels by piercing the deep layers of rock that trap them. We call them fossil fuels, because they were made from tiny plants and creatures millions of years ago. Under extreme heat and pressure, they have changed into oil and gas.

Rig
Sea level
Deck
Piles
Seafloor
Wells
Oil and gas reservoir

Mine hotspots

The world's deepest mine is South Africa's Mponeng gold mine, which plunges down 2.4 miles (3.87 km). It is so close to Earth's layer of hot magma that its temperature can reach more than 122°F (50°C). So ice slurry is piped down to the bottom, where it cools the air for the mine's 6,000 workers.

Shaft to ice pipe
Ice slurry

43

Volcano Power

A volcano forms when Earth's crust splits apart under the force of hot, molten magma rock below. Clouds of ash and sulfurous gases shoot up from the mantle layer. Magma cools in different forms, from hard, shiny swirls of pahoehoe lava to crunchy stones.

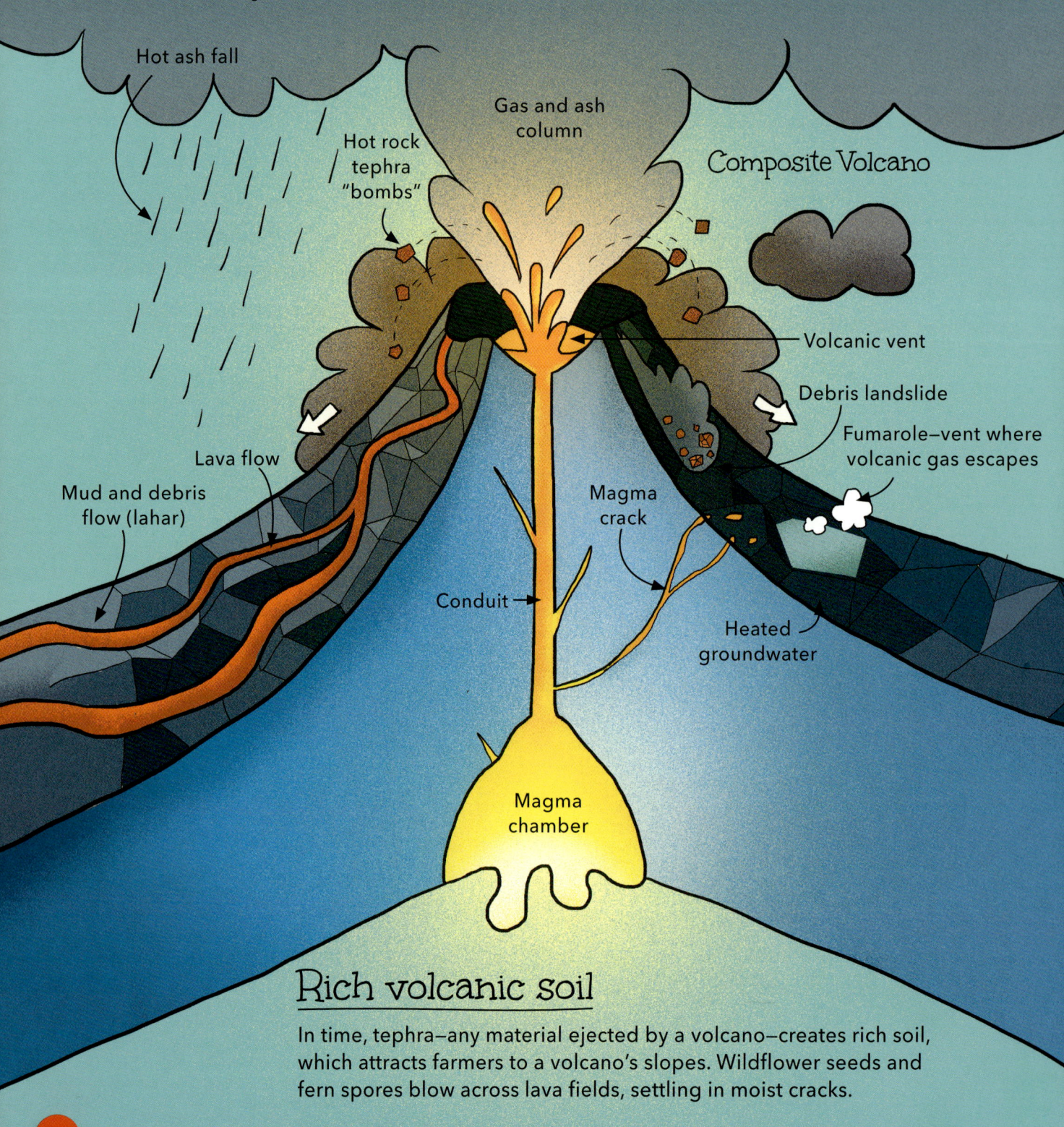

- Hot ash fall
- Gas and ash column
- Hot rock tephra "bombs"
- Composite Volcano
- Volcanic vent
- Debris landslide
- Fumarole—vent where volcanic gas escapes
- Lava flow
- Mud and debris flow (lahar)
- Magma crack
- Conduit
- Heated groundwater
- Magma chamber

Rich volcanic soil

In time, tephra—any material ejected by a volcano—creates rich soil, which attracts farmers to a volcano's slopes. Wildflower seeds and fern spores blow across lava fields, settling in moist cracks.

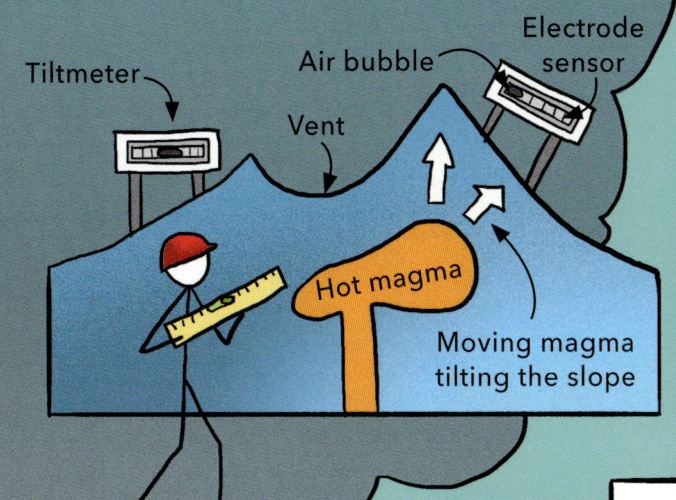

When will it erupt?

Predicting the time and force of deep volcanic explosions is a challenge. Vulcanologists place tiltmeters horizontally, high on the sides of a volcanic vent. When hot magma rises, it pushes a bulge into the vent's surface, altering the slope. The air bubble inside the tiltmeter moves, indicating an explosion will probably occur.

Mighty explosions

Most recent volcanic eruptions are measured by the amount of force generated by the explosion and the damage it caused. The Tambora eruption (see right) killed 92,000 people. With an explosive magnitude of 7 on the volcanic explosivity index (VEI), it is known as a supercolossal eruption. Damage is not limited to human casualties. Thick ash from the volcano smothers flora and crops, killing them with heat, weight, and toxins, followed by a lack of air and light.

Most Destructive Volcanoes

1. Tambora, Indonesia, 1815
2. Santorini, Greece, 1628 BCE
3. Krakatau, Indonesia, 1883
4. Santa Maria, Guatemala, 1902
5. Mount St. Helens, USA, 1980
6. Vesuvius, Italy, 79 CE
7. Pinatubo, Philippines, 1991
8. Mount Pelée, Martinique, 1902
9. Nevado del Ruiz, Colombia, 1985
10. Unzen, Japan, 1792

Living on gases

Down on the ocean floor, hot toxic gases, such as hydrogen sulfide, shoot up through volcanic vents. Deep-sea cameras have filmed amazing life forms, such as the scaly-foot snail, surviving well on the gases. Sharks have been seen inside the underwater Kavachi volcano near the Solomon Islands in the South Pacific Ocean.

45

Smashing Plates

Enormous cracks divide Earth's crust into a jigsaw of tectonic plates. These float on the soft asthenosphere layer, which sits at the top of the thick mantle. The plates move slowly, up to 4 inches (10 cm) a year, and where their boundaries meet, the crust shakes, causing earthquakes.

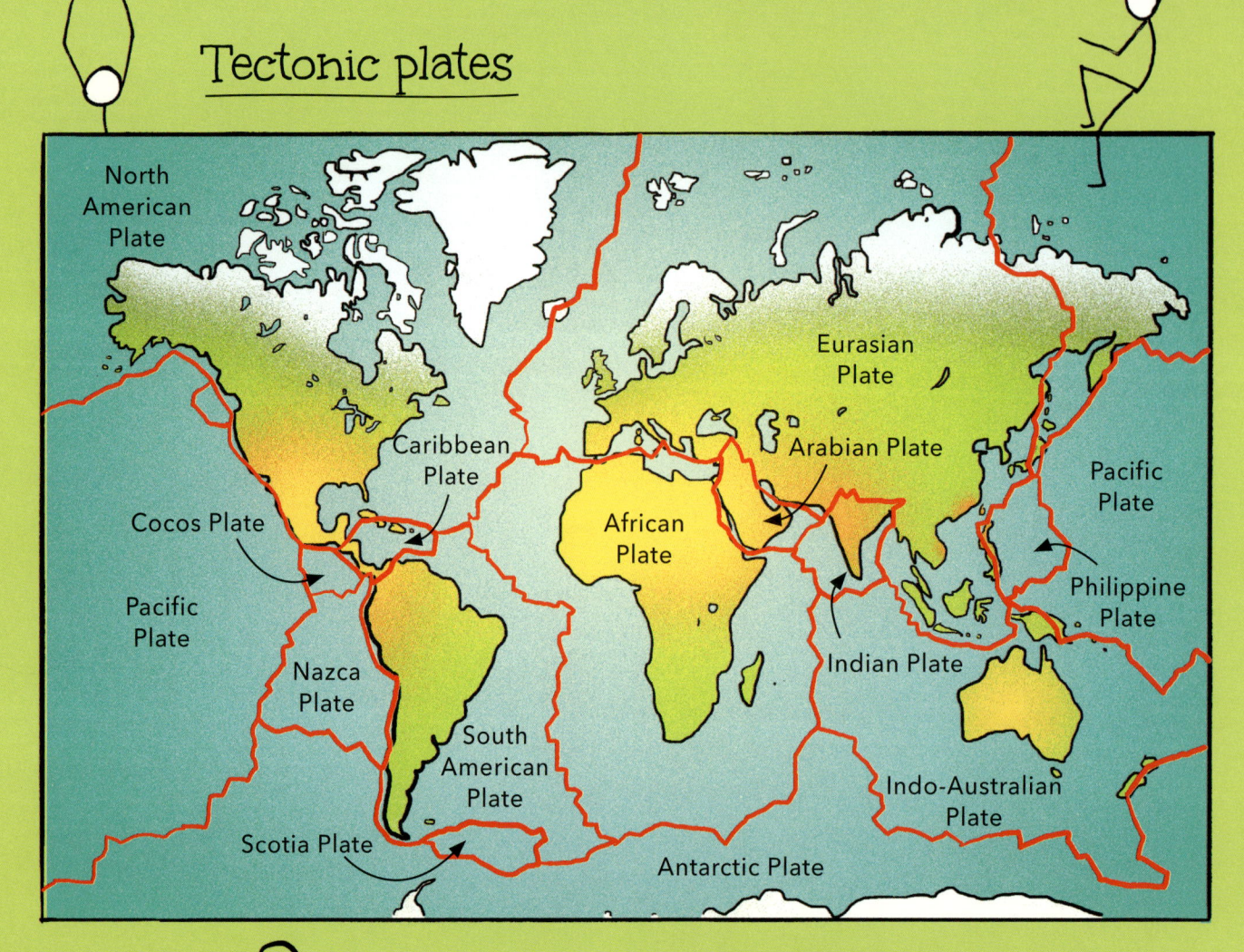

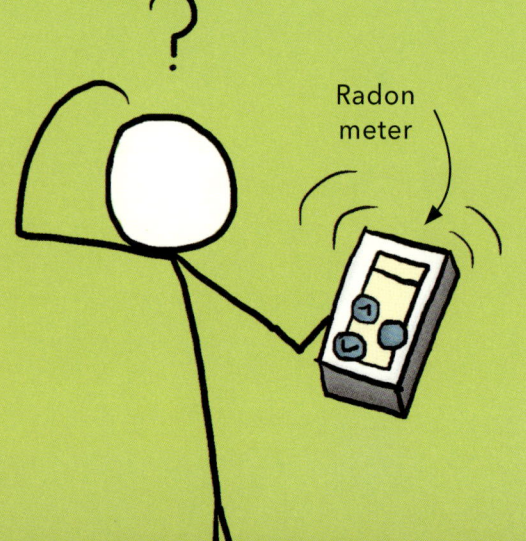

Tectonic plates

- North American Plate
- Eurasian Plate
- Caribbean Plate
- Arabian Plate
- Pacific Plate
- Cocos Plate
- African Plate
- Philippine Plate
- Pacific Plate
- Indian Plate
- Nazca Plate
- South American Plate
- Indo-Australian Plate
- Scotia Plate
- Antarctic Plate

Radon meter

Warning signs

Earthquake prediction is difficult and not very successful. This handheld meter measures changes in radon gases released as the plates move. Seismometers measure Earth's tremors, while laser beams set across fault lines register movement. Changes in water table levels, stream flows, and even animal behavior are also monitored.

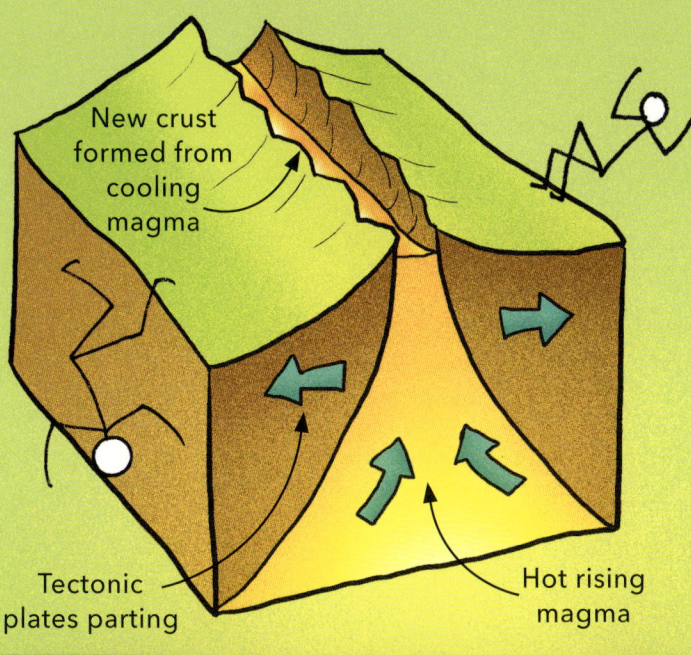

How our Earth moves

Tectonic plates interact with each other in different ways to cause earthquakes. They might slowly collide or slide against each other, grating as they move. Sometimes tremors are caused when the plates move apart or when one pushes up on top of the other.

New crust formed from cooling magma

Tectonic plates parting

Hot rising magma

What happens in a quake?

Millions of years ago, massive movements of tectonic plates shaped Earth into our continents. Today, smaller plate movements can destroy buildings and entire towns. They tear cracks in roads and railroad lines, pull down bridges, and break communication links.

Measuring a quake

Earthquake vibrations are measured using seismometers. Each movement is given a value of 1 to 10 on the Richter Scale. The most destructive is 10, which indicates many deaths and a lot of destruction. But tremors can affect people far from land. Some radiate into the sea, making it swell into walls of water that crash against distant shores. These devastating waves are called tsunamis, and they kill even more people than earthquakes.

Most Destructive Earthquakes

Place	Date	Magnitude
Chile	1960	9.5
Alaska	1964	9.2
Sumatra, Indonesia	2004	9.1
Honshu, Japan	2011	9.0
Kamchatka, east Russia	1952	9.0
Chile, off Maule coast	2010	8.8
Ecuador, off coast	1906	8.8
Alaska, Rat Island	1965	8.7
Sumatra, Indonesia	2005	8.6
Tibet and Assam, India	1950	8.6

Cities

The most successful cities in the world attract millions of people. New arrivals and new businesses put pressure on land. This is why our biggest cities are built upward—and down below ground level. This book takes a look at what happens from the top to the underground depths, and the layers in between.

Reaching for the Sky
City skyscrapers soar higher and higher, but no space is wasted, even at the top! The wind, sun, and great views are used to their full potential.

High Power
From the top, elevators and escalators whisk you down from floor to floor, powered by electric cables hidden behind walls and ceilings.

Along the Ground
You can walk, cycle, or take the bus or tram along bustling city streets. Shiny store windows and dazzling neon lights make the big city sparkle.

Underground
For speedy travel, take the underground train. Also down under lie hidden networks of cabling and entire water and sewage systems.

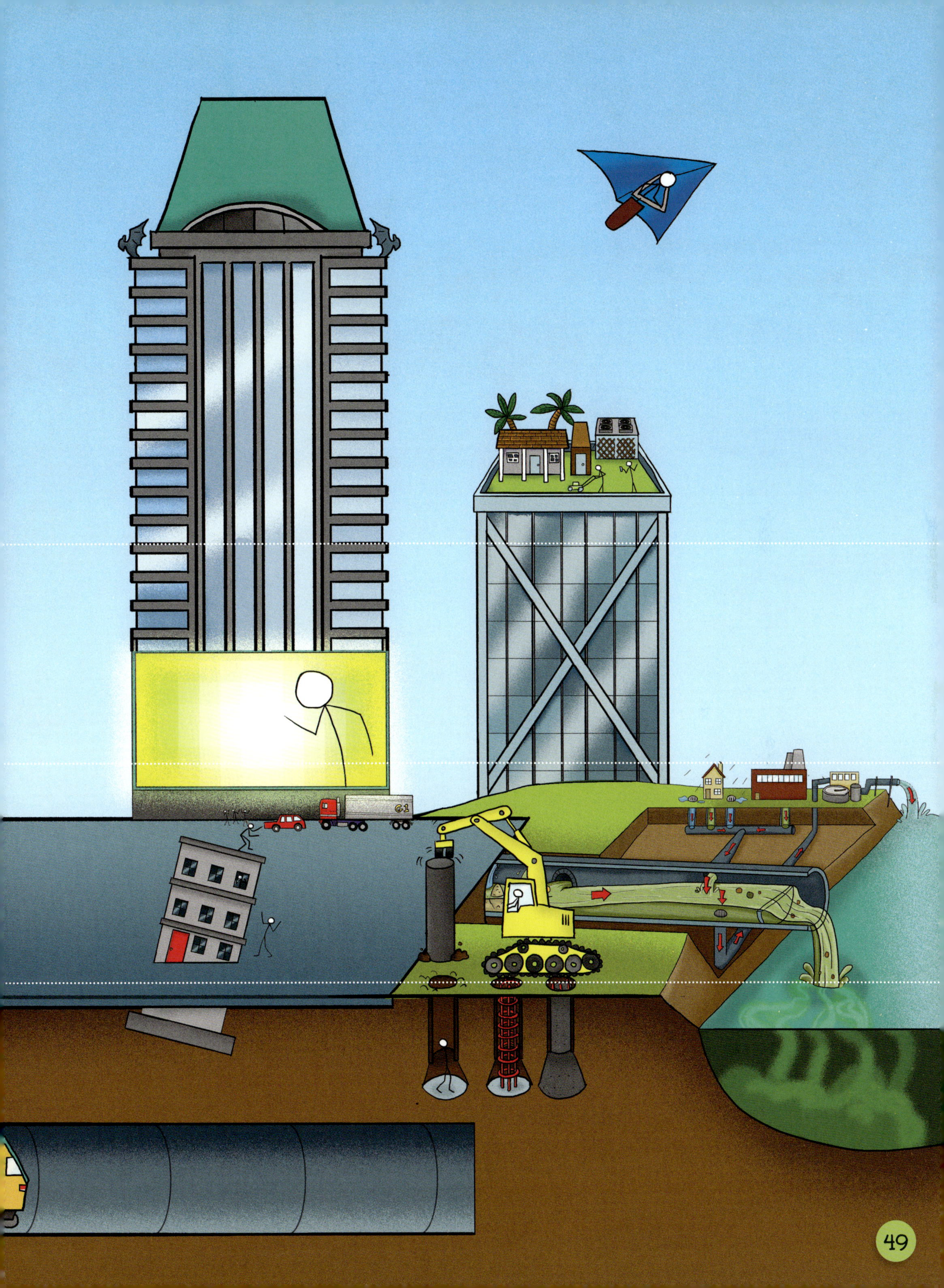
G1

On Top of the World

Architects test their skyscraper designs in wind tunnels to make sure the tops can cope with high winds. They build in curves and fins to reduce the impact. But they also make use of those dizzy heights and stiff breezes!

Satellite dishes
Communication mast

Getting the message

Communications are key to running a city. Clear signals are vital, so the tops of skyscrapers are ideal for siting telecommunications equipment. These include antennas that receive radio waves, and transmitters that emit them. Sky-high satellite dishes receive signals from satellites orbiting Earth in the upper atmosphere.

Solar panels

Soaking up the sun

The top of a tall building is the perfect place to capture the sun's energy. There are fewer tightly packed buildings to create shadows. Here, panels of photovoltaic cells (solar panels) can be positioned to get maximum exposure to the sun all day. This is a sustainable way to make electricity.

Wind turbine blades

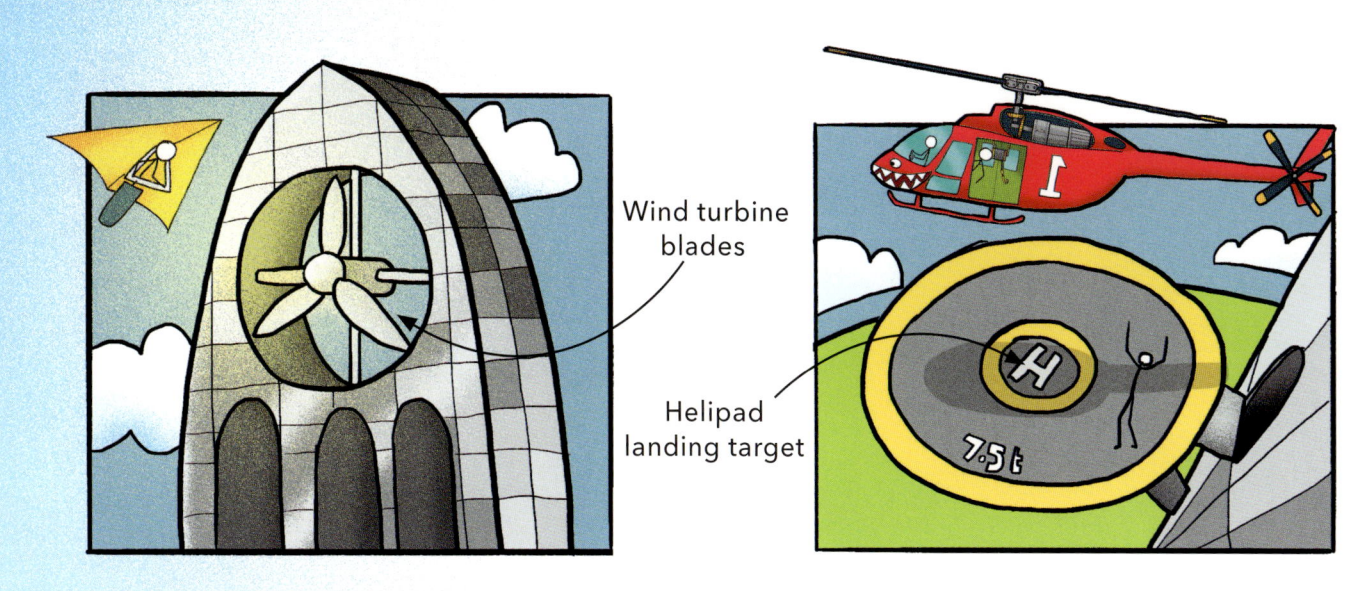

Helipad landing target

Catching the wind

This wind turbine at the top of a tower in Dubai is integrated into the building. Its clever design makes the turbine more stable in winds that reach 90 miles per hour (150 km/h). Skyscrapers in many cities worldwide have to include a sustainable source of energy in their design, as here.

High helipad

Flying in helicopters is a great way to avoid city traffic. More important, firefighters can land close to flames engulfing the tops of skyscrapers. The highest helipad is on top of China's Guangzhou International Finance Center. Here, helicopters land 1,439 feet (438 m) above the streets below.

51

Fun at the Top

Skyscrapers are expensive to build. Dubai's Burj Khalifa, the tallest building in the world, cost $1.5 billion. So investors and architects make sure that their rooftops are not wasted. They take full advantage of the view, if you dare look!

Parks in the sky

There's a lot of luxury on top of modern skyrise buildings. In Singapore, Marina Bay Sands Sky Park is a 1,115-foot (340-m)- long entertainment space. It has 250 shade trees, a 492-foot (150-m) infinity swimming pool, and restaurants overlooking the South China Sea.

Sky sports

Miniature golf courses, tennis courts, and running tracks can all be laid out on top of tall buildings, as this pitch-and-putt course has been. Sky-high sports lovers might be surprised by an urban free-climber appearing suddenly over the railings! These climbers use no safety gear to scale city skyscrapers.

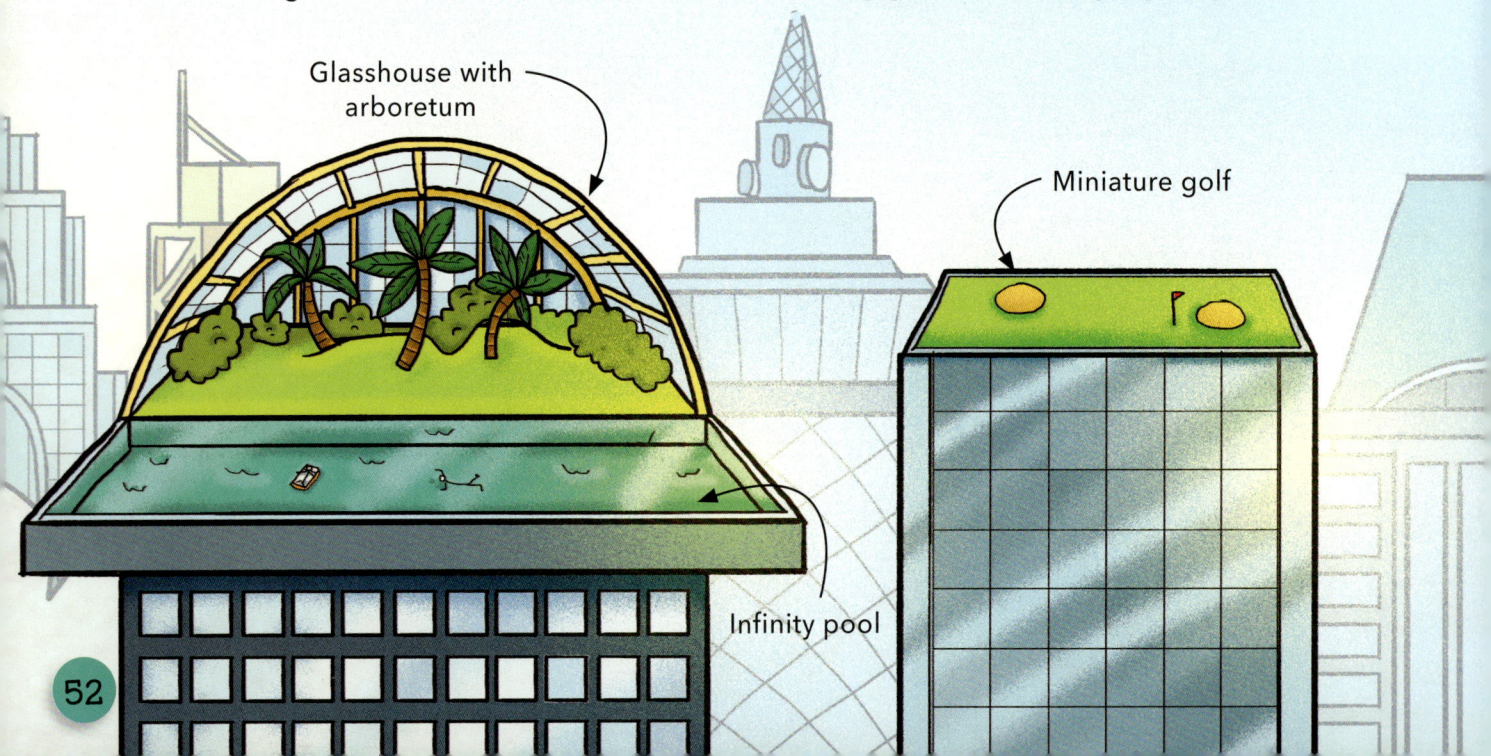

Glasshouse with arboretum

Miniature golf

Infinity pool

52

Flying fairground

Hair-raising chair rides, such as this, are suspended from skyscraper rooftops and rotate around them. Polercoaster is a high-rise roller-coaster designed with a 5,200-foot (1,584-m) track that can whiz riders around at 65 miles per hour (100 km/h). It was designed for a retail complex in Orlando, Florida.

Greening the city
Plants grown in rooftop gardens help to absorb cities' polluting gases. They release more oxygen into the air for people to breathe, too.

Air-conditioning unit

Shed

Sunroom

Lawn

Sheds on top

High-rise roofs are not always topped by sleek restaurants and pools. Among air-conditioning vents and water tanks, some city dwellers build ramshackle sheds, sunrooms, greenhouses, vegetable beds, and even beehives. Some rooftops are planted with succulent species that need no artificial watering.

Flying swings

53

Going Down

Skyscrapers would be unusable without elevators to take you up to the top or down to the ground. The elevators in China's CTF Finance Center in Guangzhou city can descend at 65 feet (20 m) per second!

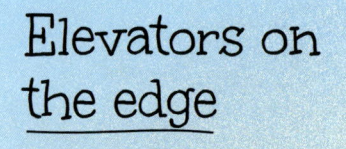

Elevators on the edge

Elevators take up precious space inside narrow city buildings. So some are built on the outside, such as this one on the Lloyds Building in London, England.

Double-deckers

Skyscrapers can house thousands of people, who line up at elevators during morning and evening rush hours. Double-decker elevators (left) that move both people and goods have helped solve the problem. They have two separate cabs in one unit and stop on two floors at the same time. The first building to install these was the 110-story Sears Tower in Chicago in 1973. Engineers are now designing triple-decker elevators.

54

Carbon-fiber cable

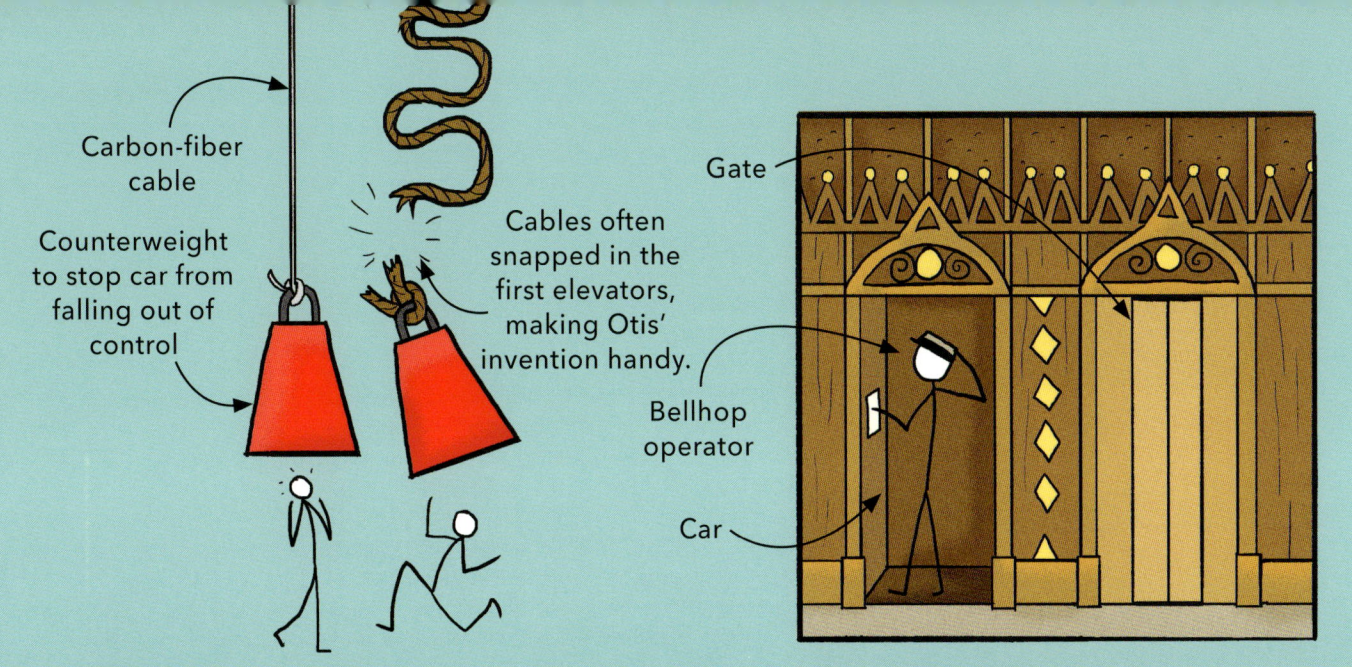

Counterweight to stop car from falling out of control

Cables often snapped in the first elevators, making Otis' invention handy.

Gate

Bellhop operator

Car

Supercables

Tough steel cables raise and lower most elevators today. But superstrong, lightweight carbon-fiber cables, and belts coated with tough polyurethane, are being developed to replace them. Engineers are designing new braking systems to serve skyscrapers 3,300 feet (1,000 m) tall. Elevators can drop at 65 feet per second (20 m/sec)—that's 45 miles per hour (72 km/h).

The first elevator

Elevator design dates to 236 BCE in ancient Greece. But American Elisha Graves Otis introduced the first safety elevator in 1854. It was a spring-loaded device that caught the platform if it fell. In the twentieth century, piston-powered hydraulic elevators were designed for low-rise buildings.

Hydraulic elevator

Display with floor number

Car

Automatic door

Shaft

Hydraulic piston that moves the elevator

Hydraulic pump

Hydraulic cylinder

Testing, testing

Engineers use computer simulation to design the lofty elevators of the future. But in Finland, the Kone company has plunged a 1,000-foot (305-m) test elevator shaft down into a limestone mine. Here, experimental elevators are tested at speeds of up to 56 feet per second (17 m/sec).

55

High Power

Bright city lights that reach to the rooftops need constant power. So do vital safety systems, such as fire alarms, sprinklers, CCTV cameras, and burglar alarms. Offices need power and fiber-optic cables for computer and Internet links.

Patch panel

High wire

Electricians access patch panels between floors and ceilings to install and service power and communication hubs. These are connected to wiring threaded upward behind the walls.

The largest screen

Brightly lit screens advertising stores and shows dazzle high above city streets everywhere. New York City's Times Square boasts a screen that spans a whole block. It stretches from 45th Street to 46th Street, is eight stories high, and gleams with nearly 24 million LED (Light Emitting Diode) pixels.

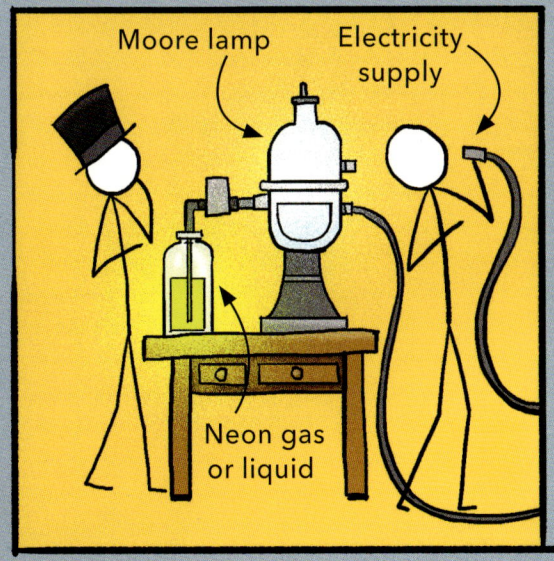

Moore lamp
Electricity supply
Neon gas or liquid

Bright lights

Tall buildings and narrow streets made cities dark at night until about 100 years ago. They lit up after Frenchman Georges Claude discovered that passing electricity through neon gas or liquid produced a bright red light. He confined the light inside a Moore lamp, and the neon light was born.

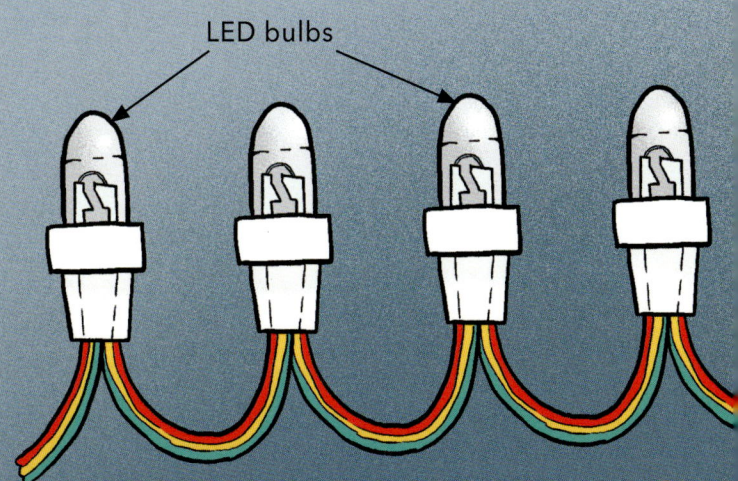

LED revolution

LEDs are bright spots of light produced by electricity, known as electroluminescence. They are often no bigger than a pinhead. Millions of these tiny red, green, and blue LED pixels together can create glowing multicolor images and words. They can move, too. LED bulbs are more energy efficient than neon or fluorescent lights and are used to illuminate streets.

LED bulbs

On the Streets

Glamorous store windows, cozy coffee shops, and bustling sidewalks make the city's ground level an attractive place. But pedestrians have to deal with cars, buses, streetcars, and bicycles streaming by. Noise and fumes fill the air in many large cities.

Living wall

Bicycle and bus lane

Living walls

City pollution is a huge health problem. Walls of plants that absorb carbon gases from vehicles help clean the air and look great, too. France's Patrick Blanc, an artist and botanist, began this trend 30 years ago. The plants are rooted to soil held in a mesh and are watered automatically.

Rattling streetcars

Streetcars are carriages on tracks, powered by electrified overhead wires. First used in Russia in the 1880s, they are quieter and cleaner than motorized vehicles. They will be even cleaner when all trams use new wire-free supercapacitors. These are stores of electricity released to power the streetcar.

Quiet tracks

Streetcar tracks clatter. So in some cities, grass is laid between the tracks to dampen the sound. The grass also absorbs carbon pollution in the air. In Rotterdam in the Netherlands, street surfaces are now made of "quiet asphalt" to reduce vehicle noise.

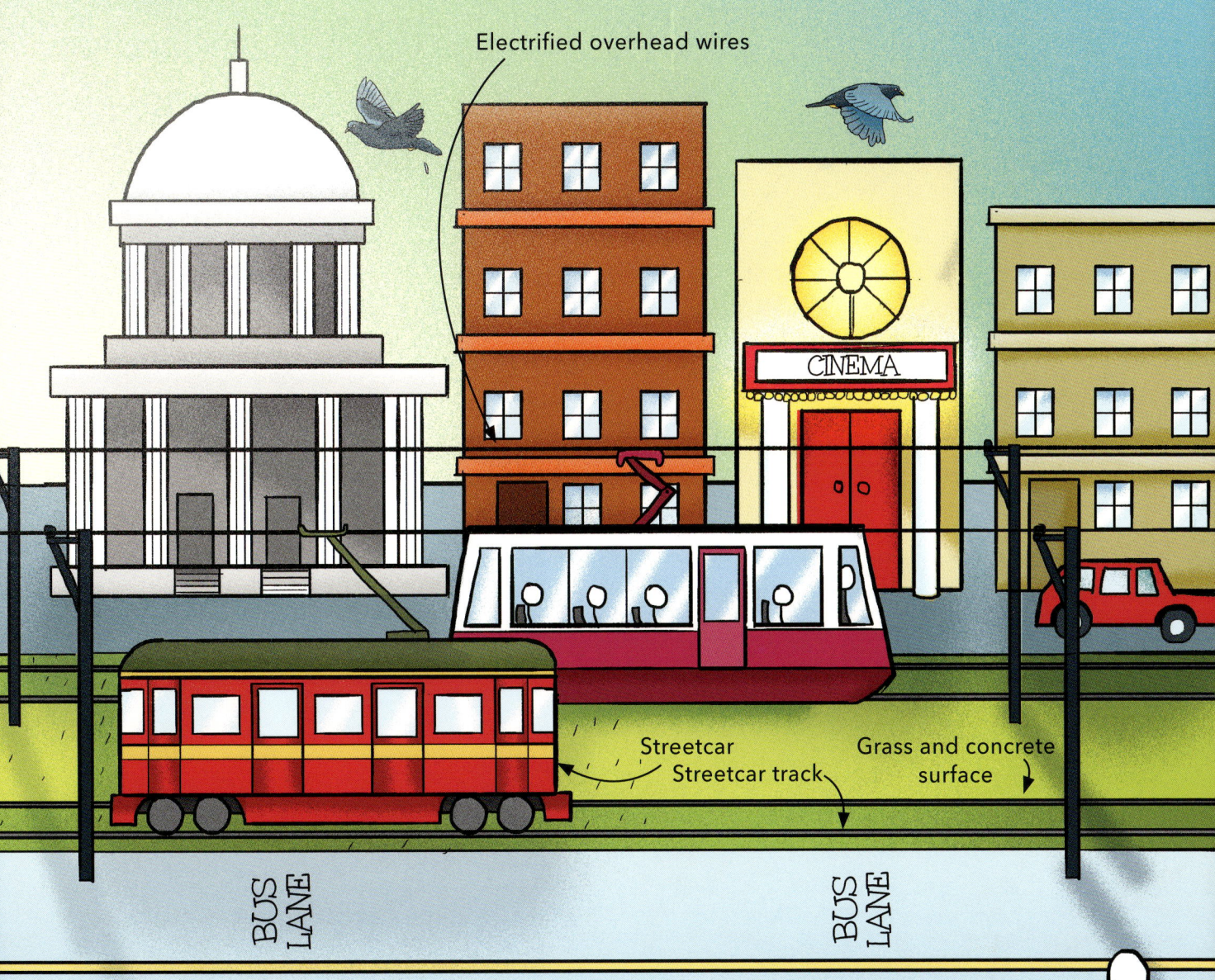

Electrified overhead wires

Streetcar
Streetcar track

Grass and concrete surface

BUS LANE

BUS LANE

Flood danger

Heavy rain runs off the city's hard concrete and asphalt surfaces, filling drains and flooding streets. Grasscrete (openwork concrete paving with grass centers) lets water soak away.

Openwork concrete shapes with porous grass pockets

Power under Our Feet

Below the city streets, networks of cables bring light, heat, and communications to billions of people. Above ground, these wires would be exposed to snow, ice, and high winds. The first underground cabling was laid 150 years ago.

The price of power

Installing power below our streets can be dangerous work and disrupts busy pedestrians. It is also expensive. Underground electric cables cost between five and ten times more to install than those above ground. Repairing them can cost 60 percent more.

Bending light

Office computers and cash registers operate by using signal transmitters called optical fibers. These thin tubes of high-quality glass carry information as light rays that seem to "bend" as they move, by bouncing along the tubes.

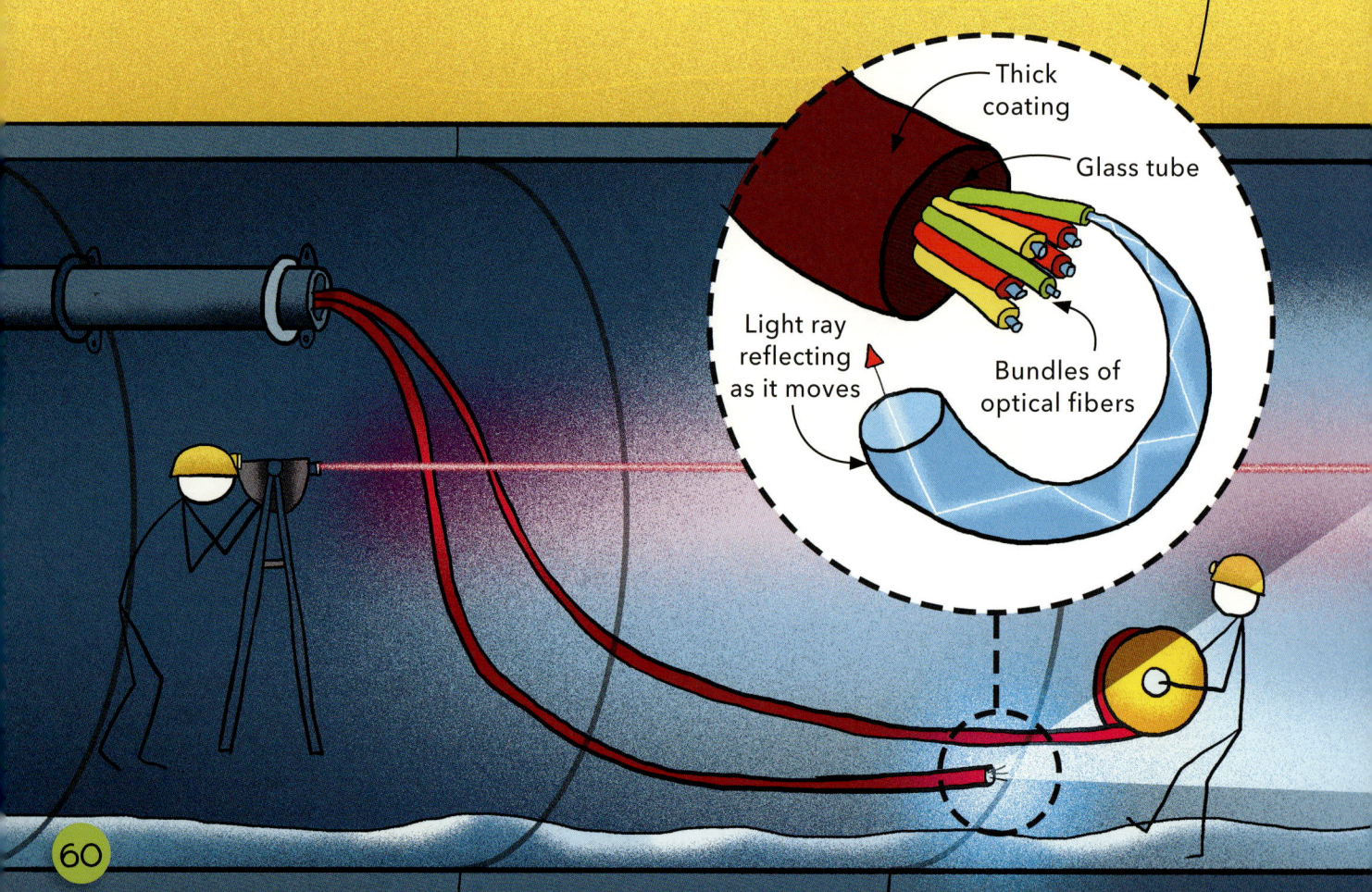

Thick coating

Glass tube

Light ray reflecting as it moves

Bundles of optical fibers

Laying cables

Cables are pushed into position using rods or pulled by winches. The jetting technique pushes cables through with a rush of air. This helps to stop them from sticking against pipes or other cables. "Floating" the cables in a stream of water prevents buckling and bending as they are fed through.

Cable-pushing machine

Live electricity wire

Gnaw, really?

When power is cut, engineers often find that the cable jackets have been gnawed through. This is the work of mice, rats, and gophers trying to sharpen their teeth. Solutions include a steel coating on the cables, or treating them with capsaicin, a burning chemical found in chili peppers.

Cable casing or ducting

Digging deep

Our growing cities need more and more cable networks. It means digging farther down or expanding the tunnels that carry them. Engineers must then make sure the cables can take the increased pressure from above. They do this with heavy insulation, pipes, and ducting around the cables.

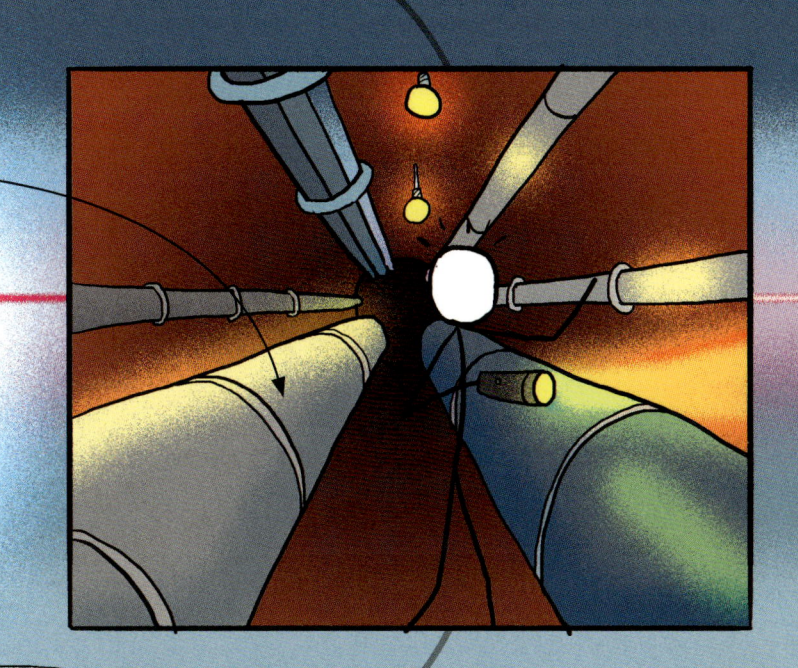

61

Keeping Clean

Deep underground, millions of gallons of water are pumped up into the city, where it is used in all kinds of ways, then drained away again. Underground sewage systems were first developed in the ancient cities of the Indus Valley (now in Pakistan) in 2500 BCE.

Rising water

In a flood, water gushes through sewers and up into the streets. Many cities are built on the coast or on river floodplains, and they are expanding. This puts pressure on both the water table (the underground water level) and pumps that carry away excess water. Excessive rainfall during torrential storms will push a city's sewage system to its limits.

Facing fatbergs

Fatbergs are huge balls of fat that slow the flow of our sewage systems. They solidify from cooking fats washed down millions of sinks. In 2013, a sewage worker in Kingston, England, found a fatberg as big as two African elephants. It was 95 percent the height of the sewer pipe itself.

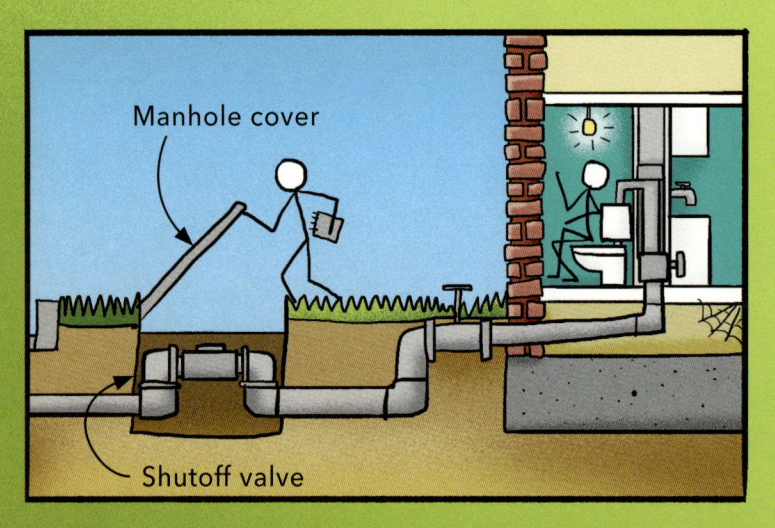

Fatberg containing waste

Stop that leak!

Leaking pipes, or water line breaks, in the water system are a costly waste. In the United States, $2.8 billion a year is spent fixing them. Water engineers access pipes through cast iron manhole covers set into sidewalks. They close shutoff valves between lengths of supply pipes to find which one is broken.

Manhole cover

Shutoff valve

Sewage and Storm Drain System

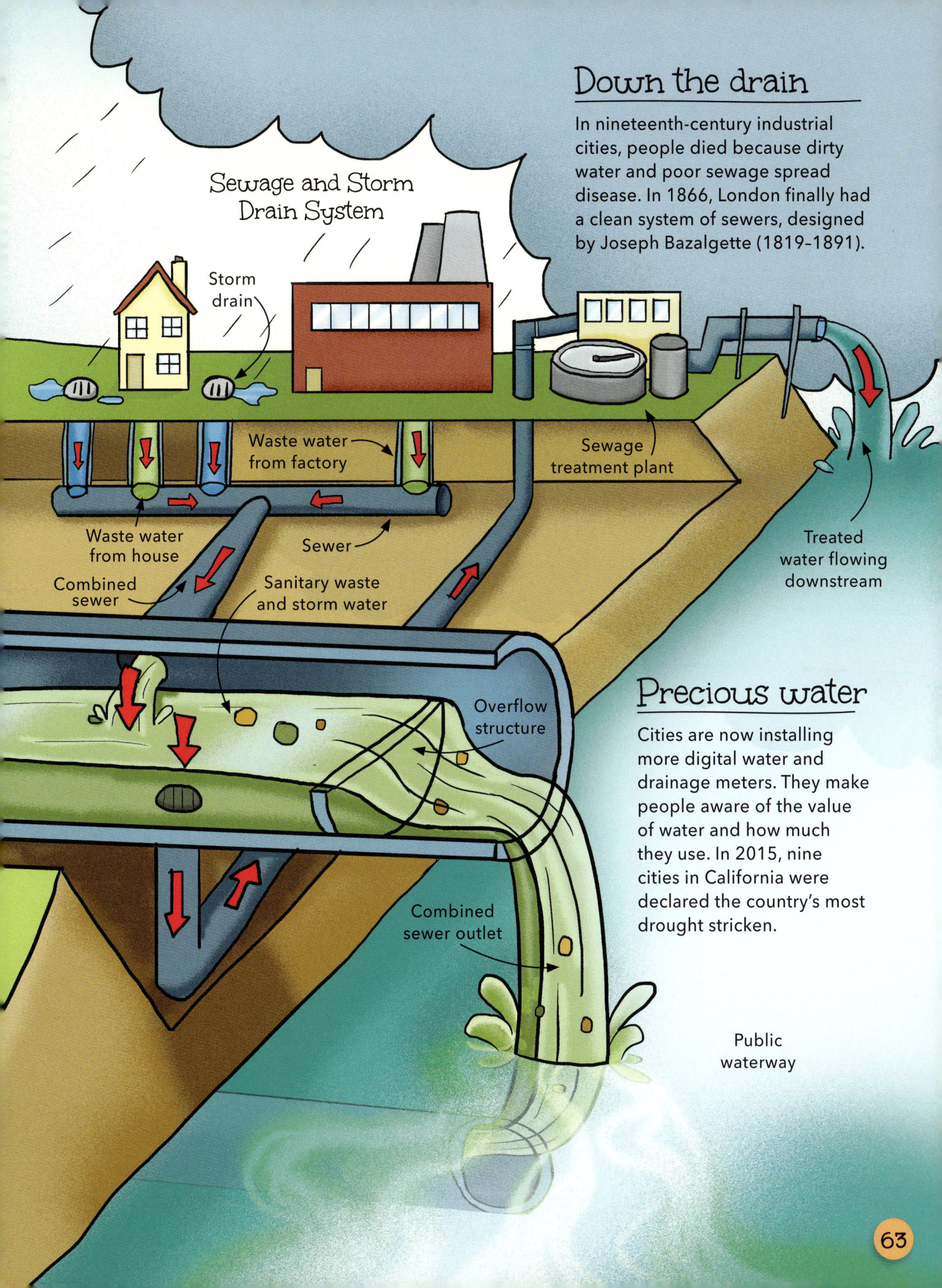

- Storm drain
- Waste water from factory
- Sewage treatment plant
- Waste water from house
- Sewer
- Combined sewer
- Sanitary waste and storm water
- Overflow structure
- Combined sewer outlet
- Treated water flowing downstream
- Public waterway

Down the drain

In nineteenth-century industrial cities, people died because dirty water and poor sewage spread disease. In 1866, London finally had a clean system of sewers, designed by Joseph Bazalgette (1819-1891).

Precious water

Cities are now installing more digital water and drainage meters. They make people aware of the value of water and how much they use. In 2015, nine cities in California were declared the country's most drought stricken.

Travel Below Ground

Underground metros, or subways, help ease traffic jams and packed sidewalks in the streets above. One of the most modern is in Denmark—Copenhagen's subway runs for 24 hours with driverless trains.

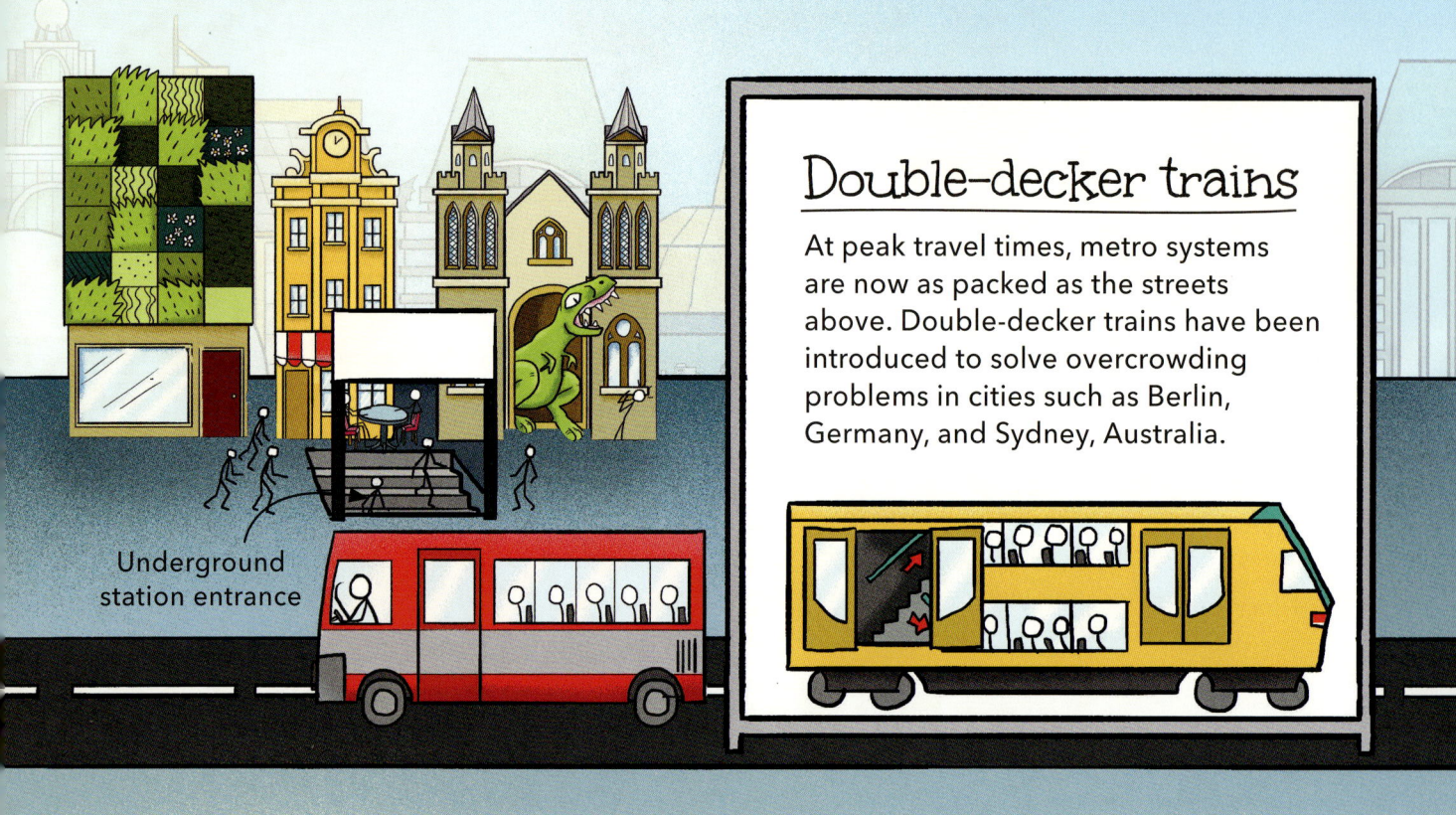

Underground station entrance

Double-decker trains

At peak travel times, metro systems are now as packed as the streets above. Double-decker trains have been introduced to solve overcrowding problems in cities such as Berlin, Germany, and Sydney, Australia.

Escalator

Early tunnel boring machine (TBM)

Tunneling a tube

The invention of hefty tunnel boring machines (TBMs) made it possible to carve out the first underground. Today's TBMs are surprisingly similar in design, but much longer, like a factory in a tube. In London, the new Crossrail underground needed eight TBMs, each about as long as two Airbus 380 airliners. They dug down 131 feet (40 m) beneath the streets.

First metro

In 1890, the City and South London Railway opened the world's first deep-level, electrified underground railroad, or metro. A masterpiece of engineering, it ran from north to south London through a tunnel built under the Thames River. The locomotives were small to fit the narrow tunnels and could haul three carriages at speeds of up to 25 miles per hour (40 km/h).

Subway facts box

Most stations	New York City (422)
Most lines	New York City (24)
Longest track	Shanghai, China 334 miles (538 km)
Most passengers	Beijing, China (more than 10 million a day)
Deepest station	Arsenalna station in Kiev, Ukraine (351 feet/107 m)

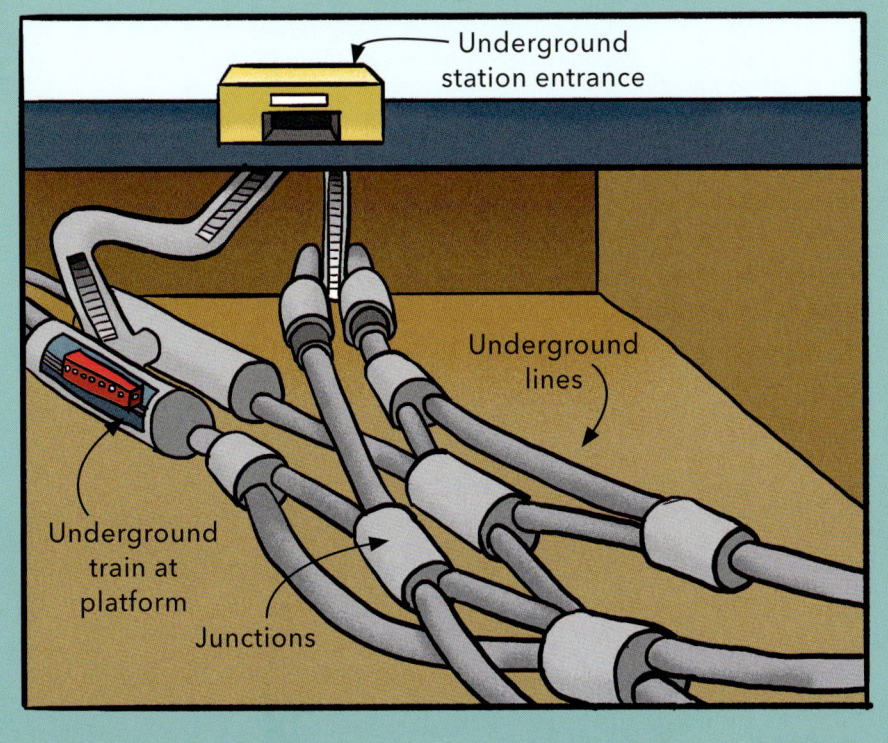

Underground station entrance
Underground lines
Underground train at platform
Junctions

Planning the lines

Subway lines converging on a single station require careful planning. Junctions join lines as they approach a platform. Here, signals stop trains on different lines from accessing a platform at the same time. New lines weave through existing ones, avoiding sewers, power supplies, and underground rivers.

Down Under

Foundations reach down to the deepest layer of our cities. They support the increasing number and height of multistory buildings. New foundation technologies allow for construction on what was once seen as unstable, unsuitable land.

Caisson pile

Steel rod reinforcement

Pile walls made of steel

Floating foundation

Bedrock   Soil

Sinking feeling

Soft soil makes normal foundations sink. But large, flat floating foundations that support high-rise buildings let them just shift slightly as the ground gives way. Clay is a soft soil, but only when wet. When dry, it shrinks, causing buildings above to subside. So deep supporting piles are driven below the clay.

Pushing down piles

Tall buildings are held up by long supports called piles, which are driven by machinery into the bedrock. Caissons are massive cylindrical piles reinforced by steel rods. They are at least 3 feet 3 inches (1 m) in diameter. Steel sheet pile walls help keep soil and rubble around them from shifting.

Deepest foundations

Malaysia's Petronas Twin Towers soar 1,483 feet (452 m) above street level. They are so tall that their pinnacles house aircraft warning lights. They sit on foundations of reinforced concrete held up by 104 supporting rods, or piles. Some of these reach down 374 feet (114 m) and are the deepest in the world.

Hitting water

The water table is the natural level of water beneath us. In many cities, foundations that are in contact with the water table push the level up, so it might lie only a few feet below. On construction sites, pumps remove excess water constantly. The basements of buildings can then be built from concrete encased by steel as a barrier to water.

Rocking with the shock

Buildings set on rigid foundations crack in an earthquake. So new skyscrapers are designed to rock with the shock waves. They rest on foundations fitted with isolators, or flexible pads, that lift or "isolate" them above the ground and let them lean. At the top of the building, if it lurches too much to one side, a heavy weight swings in a harness to rebalance the structure.

Steel bracing for strength

Foundation's isolator

Oceans

Earth's oceans are vast connected bowls of dark basalt rock. They cover 72 percent of the world and provide 70 percent of our oxygen. These oceans filled with water that was created by gaseous clouds billowing over prehistoric Earth. Ocean crusts began to form less than 200 million years ago and now hold water at an average depth of 13,000 feet (4,000 m).

The Sunlight Zone
From the sunny surface to about 660 feet (200 m) deep—the continental shelf slopes down gently at this level

The Twilight Zone
From 660 feet (200 m) to 3,300 feet (1,000 m), with faint light—the continental slope dips deep into the ocean

The Midnight Zone
From 3,300 feet (1,000 m) to 13,100 feet (4,000 m), where creatures adapt to darkness and heavy water pressure

The Abyss
From 13,100 feet (4,000 m) to 19,700 feet (6,000 m)—the continental rise reaches gently up from the abyssal floor

The Ocean's Trenches
From 19,700 feet (6,000 m) to 36,100 feet (11,000 m), where steep, narrow valleys plunge down

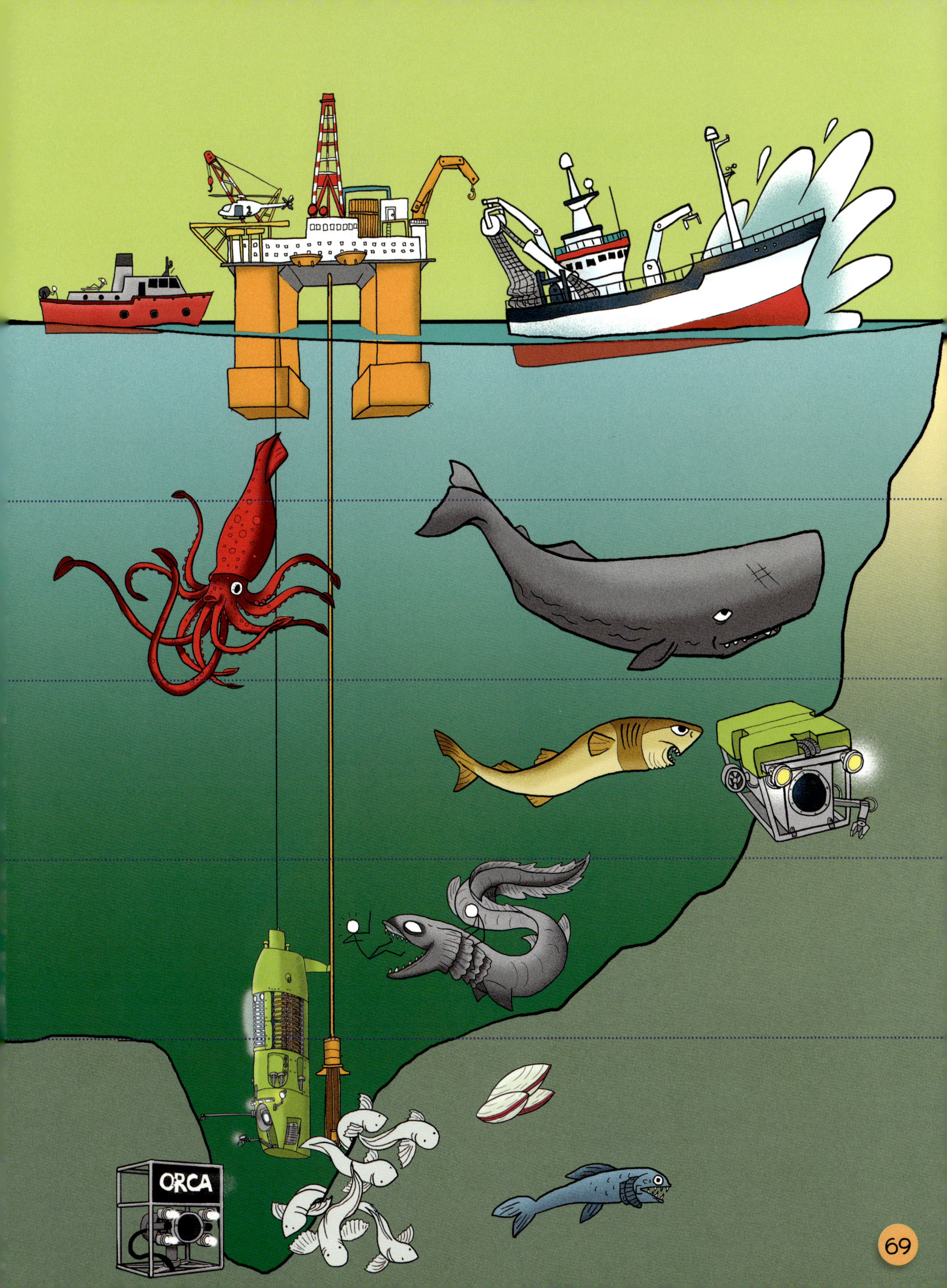
ORCA

The Sunlight Zone

In our oceans' top layer, sunlight flickers and filters through waters that teem with life. The sun's rays grow dimmer farther down the layer. But these murkier depths are still full of bright, colorful plants and creatures.

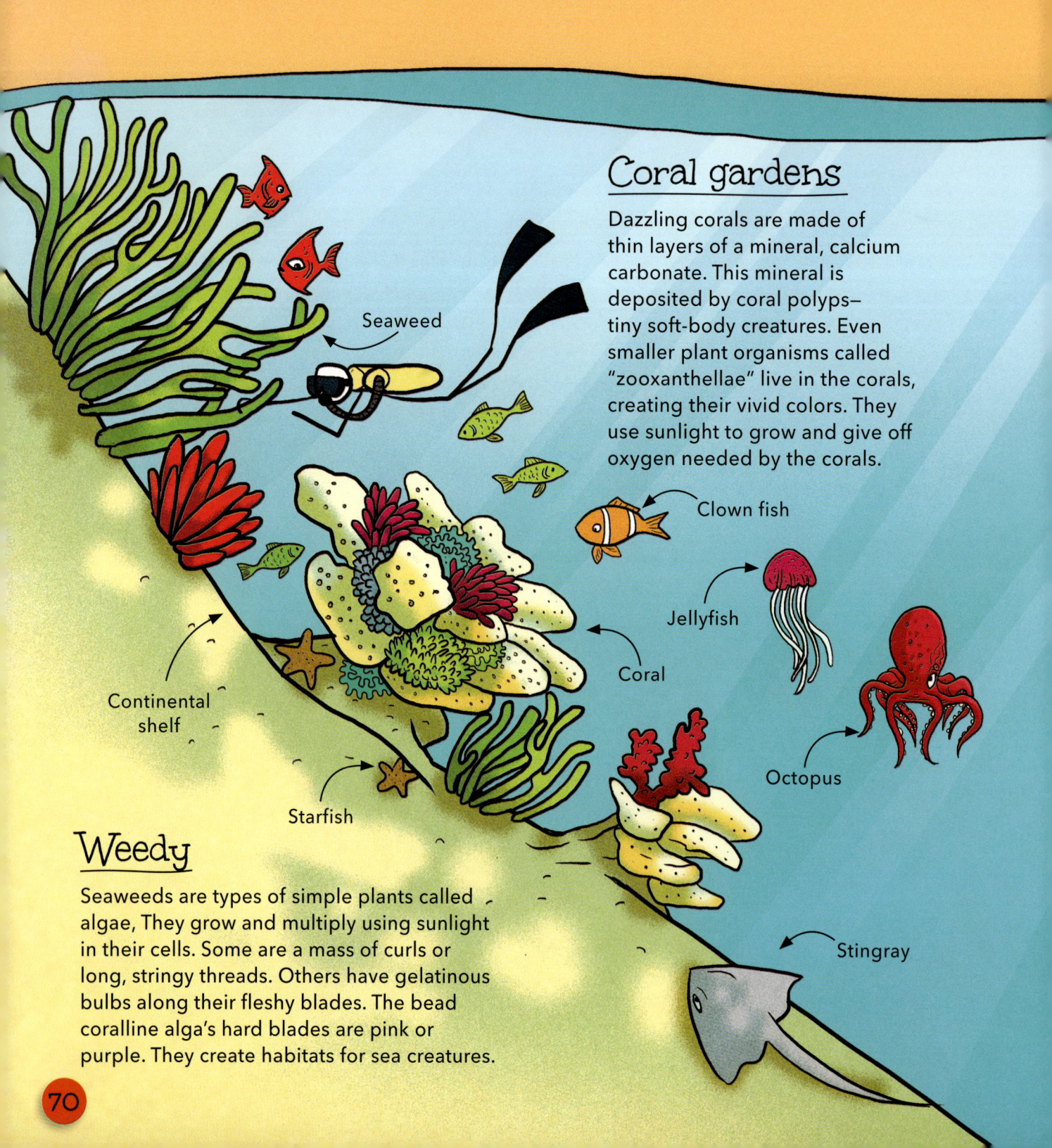

Coral gardens

Dazzling corals are made of thin layers of a mineral, calcium carbonate. This mineral is deposited by coral polyps—tiny soft-body creatures. Even smaller plant organisms called "zooxanthellae" live in the corals, creating their vivid colors. They use sunlight to grow and give off oxygen needed by the corals.

Seaweed

Clown fish

Jellyfish

Coral

Octopus

Continental shelf

Starfish

Stingray

Weedy

Seaweeds are types of simple plants called algae. They grow and multiply using sunlight in their cells. Some are a mass of curls or long, stringy threads. Others have gelatinous bulbs along their fleshy blades. The bead coralline alga's hard blades are pink or purple. They create habitats for sea creatures.

Microscopic life

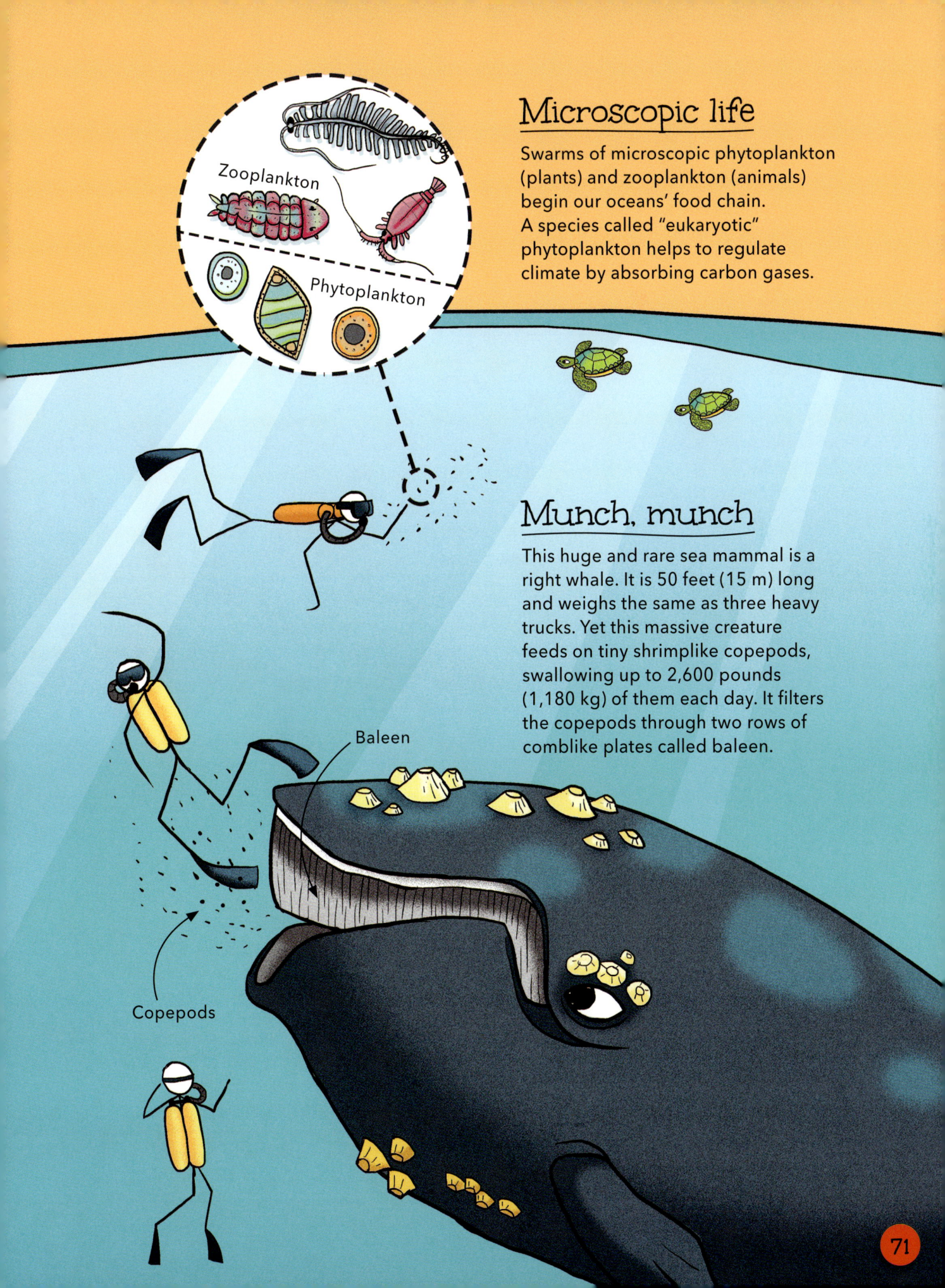

Swarms of microscopic phytoplankton (plants) and zooplankton (animals) begin our oceans' food chain. A species called "eukaryotic" phytoplankton helps to regulate climate by absorbing carbon gases.

Zooplankton

Phytoplankton

Munch, munch

This huge and rare sea mammal is a right whale. It is 50 feet (15 m) long and weighs the same as three heavy trucks. Yet this massive creature feeds on tiny shrimplike copepods, swallowing up to 2,600 pounds (1,180 kg) of them each day. It filters the copepods through two rows of comblike plates called baleen.

Baleen

Copepods

Superhighway

The sunlight zone is a well-used highway for humans. We design gigantic vessels to transport vast quantities of goods across it, from port to distant port. We fish in it, exploit its riches, and extract oil from its depths.

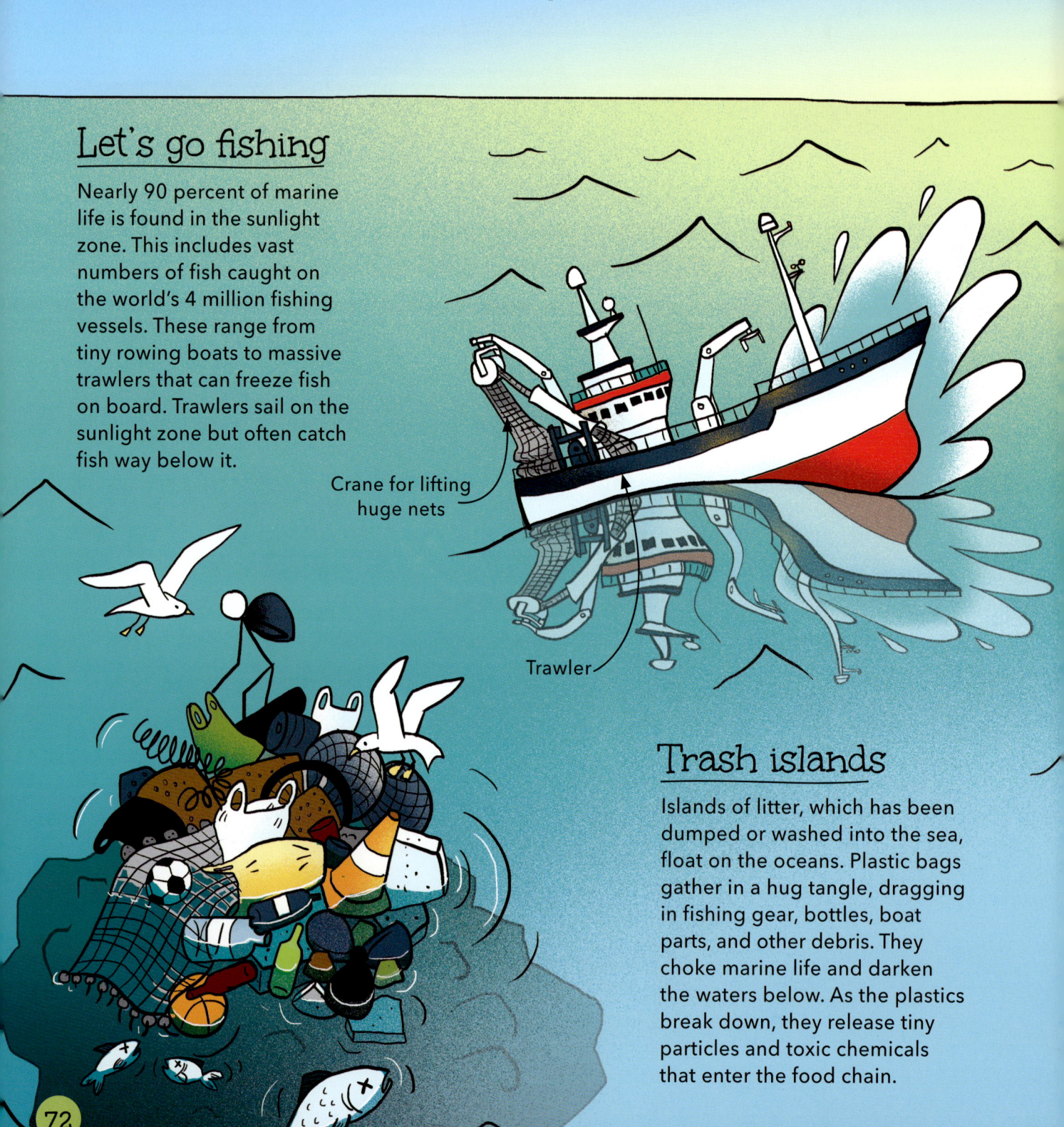

Let's go fishing

Nearly 90 percent of marine life is found in the sunlight zone. This includes vast numbers of fish caught on the world's 4 million fishing vessels. These range from tiny rowing boats to massive trawlers that can freeze fish on board. Trawlers sail on the sunlight zone but often catch fish way below it.

Crane for lifting huge nets

Trawler

Trash islands

Islands of litter, which has been dumped or washed into the sea, float on the oceans. Plastic bags gather in a hug tangle, dragging in fishing gear, bottles, boat parts, and other debris. They choke marine life and darken the waters below. As the plastics break down, they release tiny particles and toxic chemicals that enter the food chain.

On the ocean wave

The first ocean-going cargo ships were galleys. They began to sail from the Mediterranean Sea into the Atlantic Ocean in about 1280 BCE. Goods could then reach northern Europe more easily than across mountainous lands. Ships got larger, allowing for fishing in open waters.

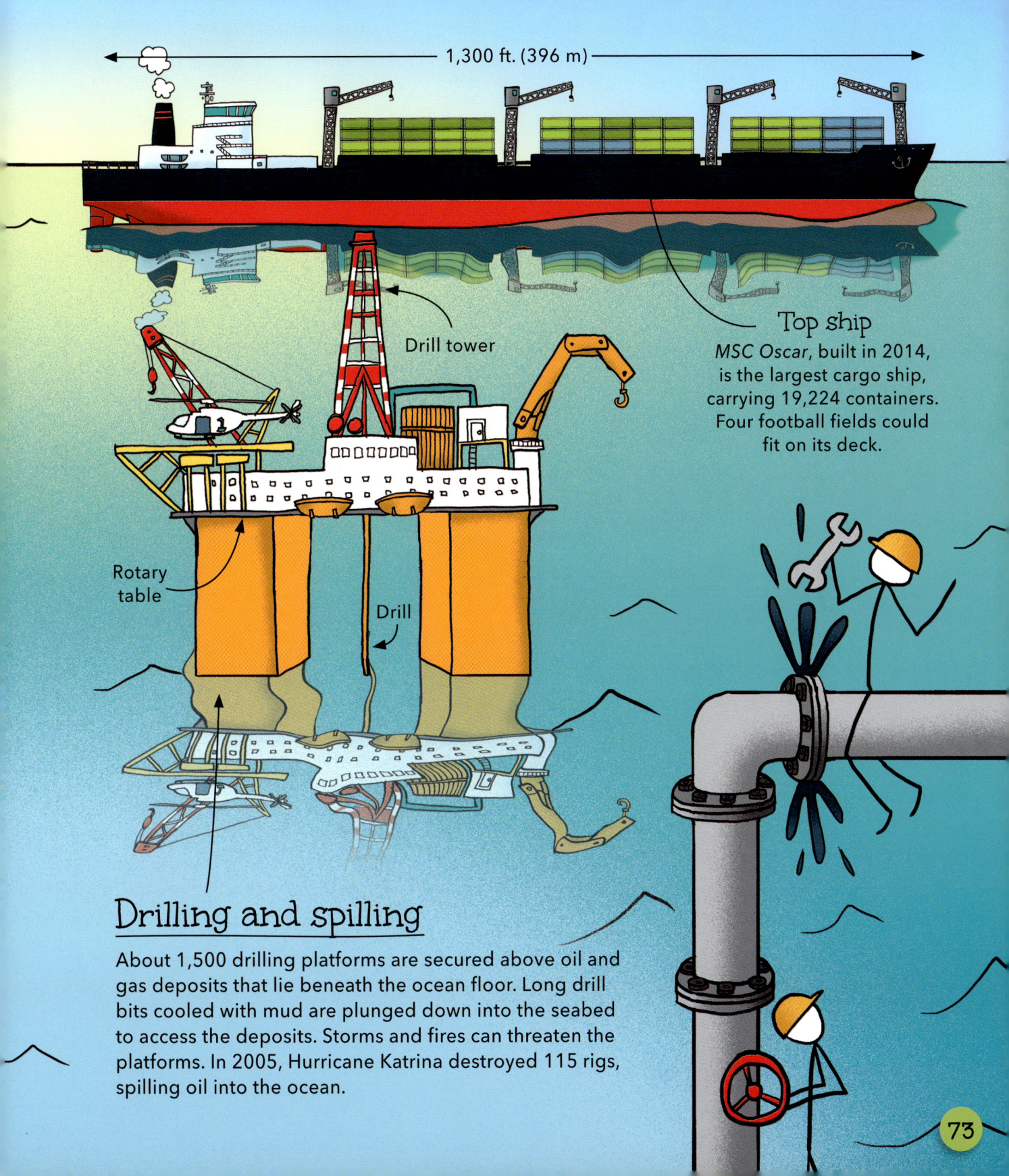

1,300 ft. (396 m)

Drill tower

Top ship
MSC Oscar, built in 2014, is the largest cargo ship, carrying 19,224 containers. Four football fields could fit on its deck.

Rotary table

Drill

Drilling and spilling

About 1,500 drilling platforms are secured above oil and gas deposits that lie beneath the ocean floor. Long drill bits cooled with mud are plunged down into the seabed to access the deposits. Storms and fires can threaten the platforms. In 2005, Hurricane Katrina destroyed 115 rigs, spilling oil into the ocean.

The Twilight Zone

The twilight zone's waters are cold and murky. Only a faint light reaches this ocean layer during the day, and everything appears a dark, indigo blue. Water pressure is high and there is little oxygen. Yet there is still plenty of life.

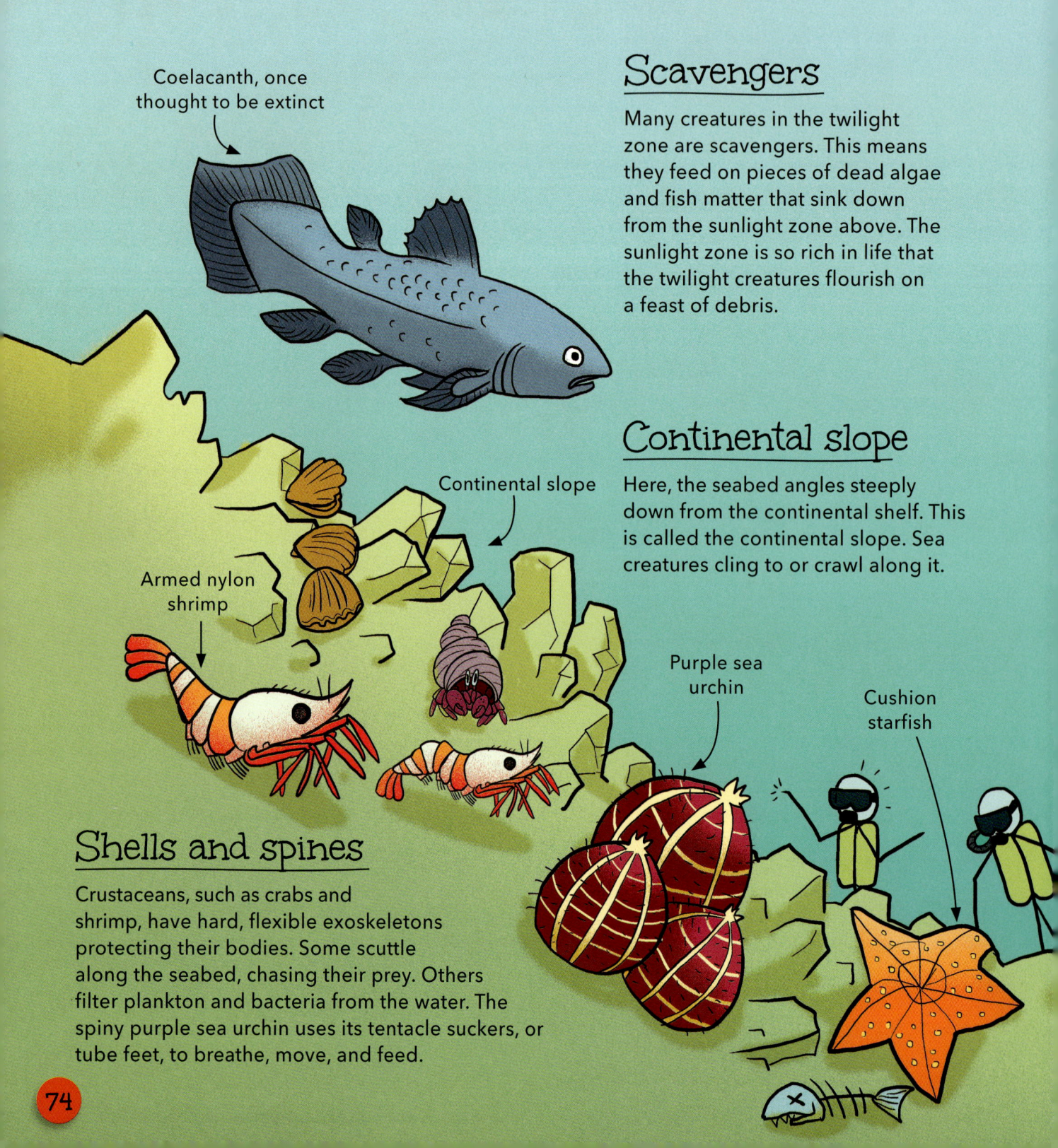

Coelacanth, once thought to be extinct

Scavengers

Many creatures in the twilight zone are scavengers. This means they feed on pieces of dead algae and fish matter that sink down from the sunlight zone above. The sunlight zone is so rich in life that the twilight creatures flourish on a feast of debris.

Continental slope

Here, the seabed angles steeply down from the continental shelf. This is called the continental slope. Sea creatures cling to or crawl along it.

Continental slope

Armed nylon shrimp

Purple sea urchin

Cushion starfish

Shells and spines

Crustaceans, such as crabs and shrimp, have hard, flexible exoskeletons protecting their bodies. Some scuttle along the seabed, chasing their prey. Others filter plankton and bacteria from the water. The spiny purple sea urchin uses its tentacle suckers, or tube feet, to breathe, move, and feed.

Squid hunt

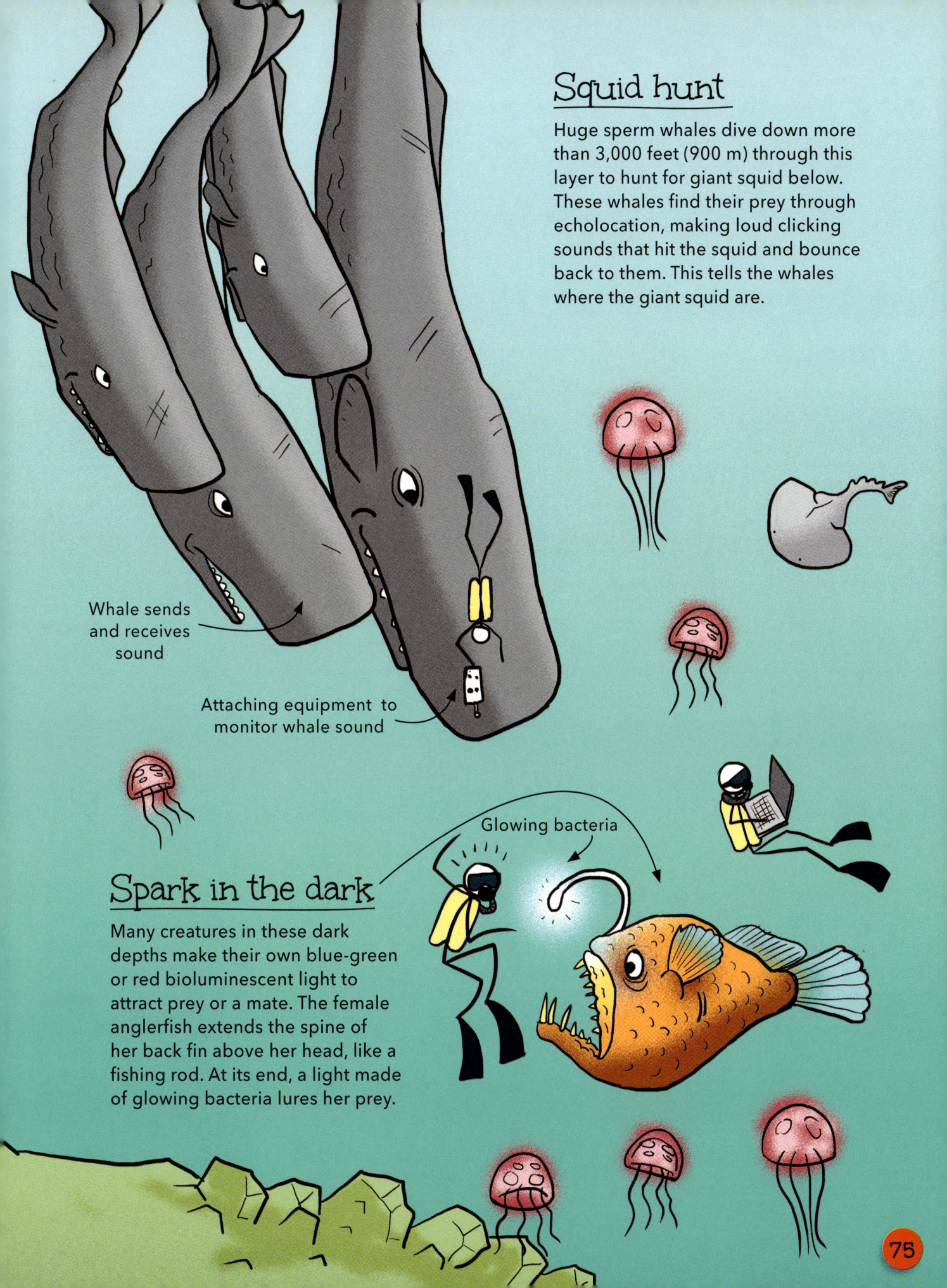

Huge sperm whales dive down more than 3,000 feet (900 m) through this layer to hunt for giant squid below. These whales find their prey through echolocation, making loud clicking sounds that hit the squid and bounce back to them. This tells the whales where the giant squid are.

Whale sends and receives sound

Attaching equipment to monitor whale sound

Glowing bacteria

Spark in the dark

Many creatures in these dark depths make their own blue-green or red bioluminescent light to attract prey or a mate. The female anglerfish extends the spine of her back fin above her head, like a fishing rod. At its end, a light made of glowing bacteria lures her prey.

Carbon sinks

Scientists lower instruments to measure the amount of carbon dioxide in the oceans. Too much carbon in the atmosphere contributes to climate change. But some ocean organisms absorb carbon dioxide, removing it from the atmosphere. The microscopic copepod excretes its carbon-trapped waste, which sinks to the oceans' depths.

PELAGRA trap for catching sediment

Marine Snow Catcher for collecting water with biological debris

Breakthrough film

Filming in the twilight zone is difficult, but in 2013 a Japanese crew took the first images of a giant squid. A team of three carried out 100 or so missions in a submersible to capture the 10-foot (3-m) cephalopod. They followed it down to around 2,900 feet (900 m).

The pressure at such depths is so huge and the territory so unknown, that the crew filmed from inside the three-man Triton submersible.

The giant squid's eyeball is the size of a dinner plate

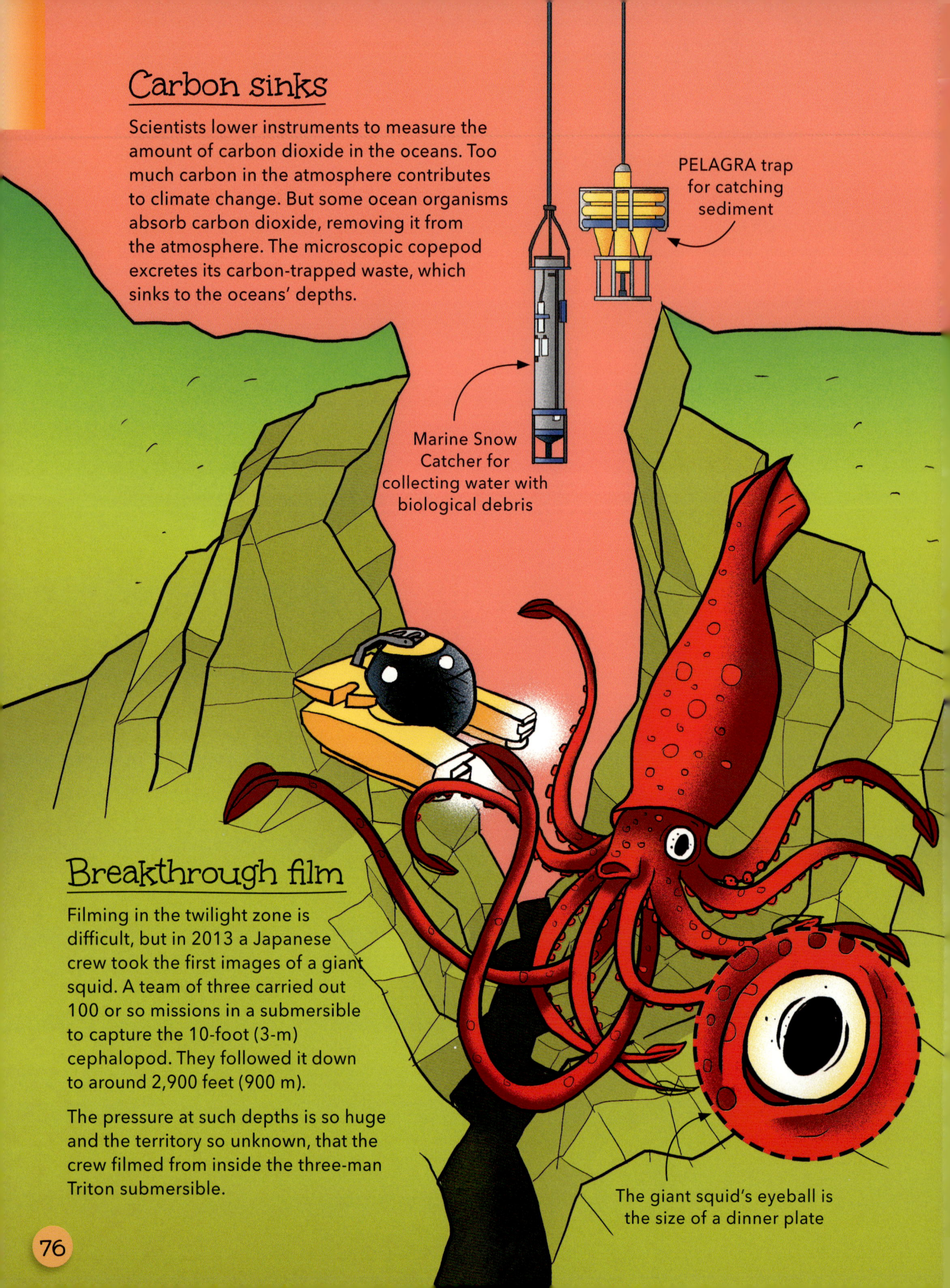

Exploring the Seabed

The twilight zone is an exciting place for oceanography, the study of our oceans. Scientists observe sea creatures, from microorganisms to the giant squid, and watch for signs of climate change on Earth.

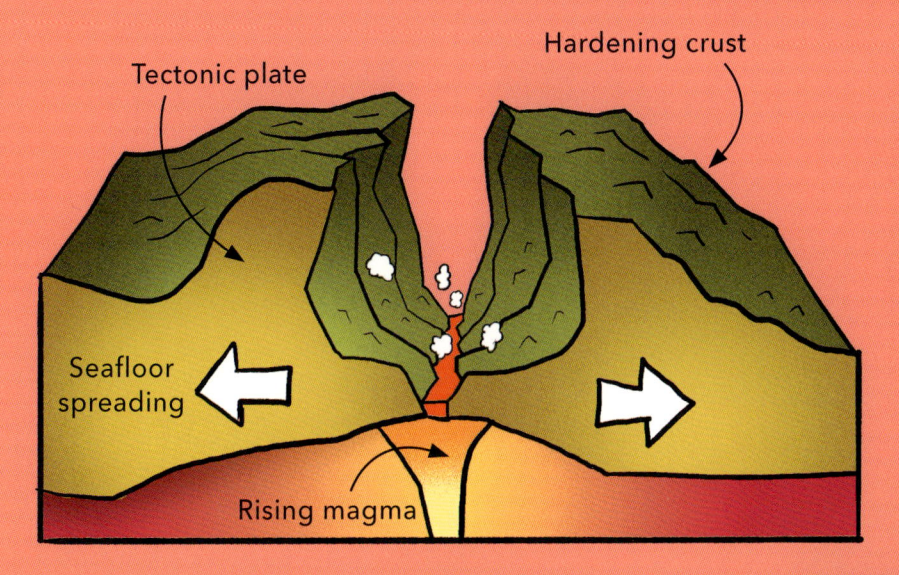

Labels: Tectonic plate, Hardening crust, Seafloor spreading, Rising magma

Mid-ocean ridge

From parts of the twilight zone to deep on the ocean floor, ridges of crusty rock lie on the edges of two great slabs of seabed. These are tectonic plates that spread apart, allowing for hot magma beneath to rise. Here, the water cools the magma to form crusty toppings. This mid-ocean ridge was not explored until 1973.

The first explorers

In 1934, scientist William Beebe (1877-1962) joined engineer Otis Barton (1899-1992) in Barton's bathysphere. The two Americans were the first to reach the twilight zone.

Labels: Oxygen supply line, 400-lb. (180-kg) door

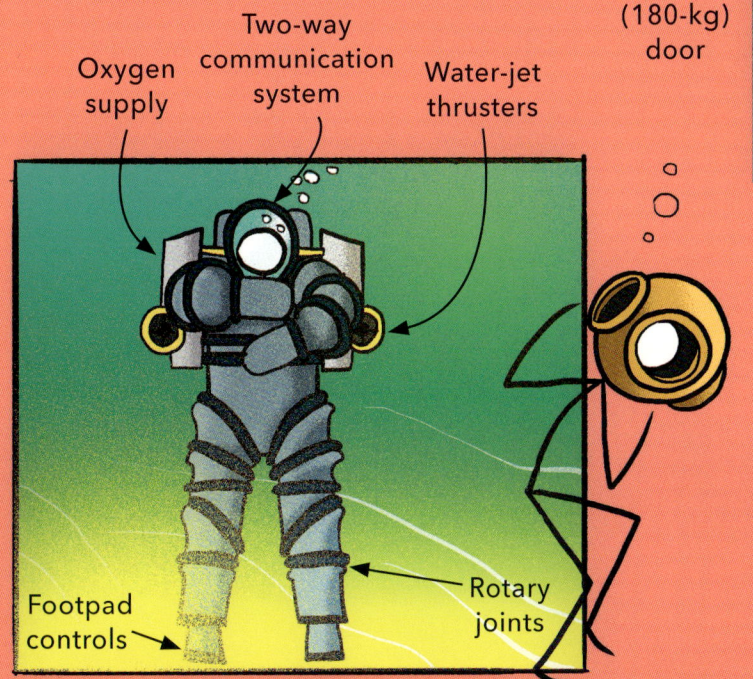

Labels: Oxygen supply, Two-way communication system, Water-jet thrusters, Footpad controls, Rotary joints

Deep-sea diving

Divers need strong suits to withstand high pressure at this level. The Exosuit (left) allows for divers to plunge 1,000 feet (300 m) below the surface. It can resist high pressure even at its weakest joints. An operator at the surface monitors conditions in the Exosuit through inbuilt links and can maneuver the suit—and the diver—away from danger.

The Midnight Zone

The chilly midnight zone occupies up to 90 percent of our oceans. The only natural light here in the deep is made by bioluminescent life forms. Many creatures are black or red to hide in the near total darkness, and some have especially large eyes—or no eyes at all.

Walking cucumbers

Sea cucumbers are echinoderms, which means they have spiny skins. They feed on debris floating in the sea or buried in the sand. Sea cucumbers move around on rows of tube feet with suckers. Some eject a tangle of threads, toxins, or even their own internal organs to put off predators.

Cuttlefish

Blobfish

Sea cucumbers

Gelatin or fish?

The gelatin-like blobfish floats just above the ocean floor in Australia's deep waters. It has almost no muscle so cannot swim. It feeds by keeping its mouth open to take in small pieces of food debris. No one has yet seen a blobfish that is more than 12 inches (30.48 cm) long.

78

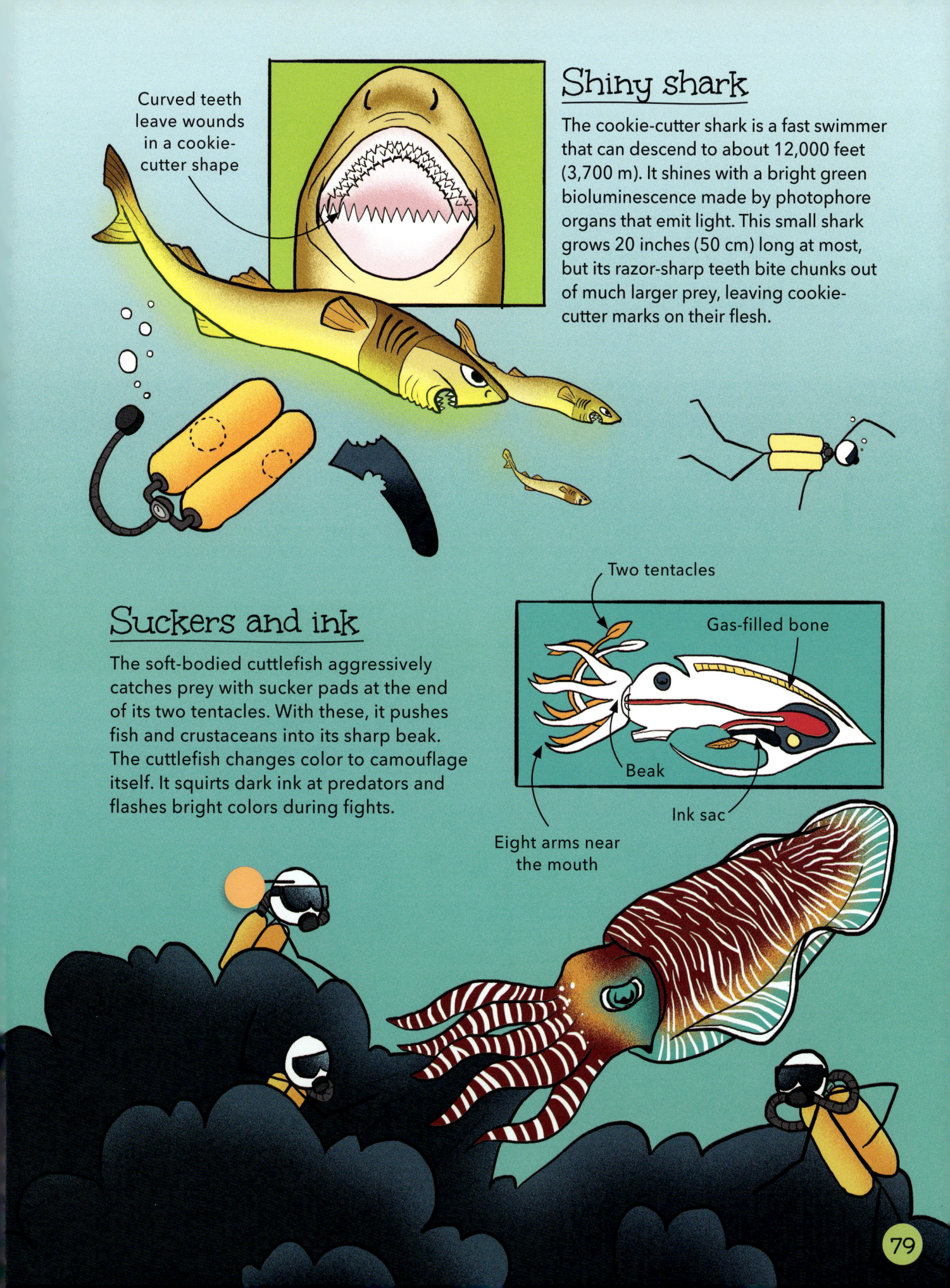

Curved teeth leave wounds in a cookie-cutter shape

Shiny shark

The cookie-cutter shark is a fast swimmer that can descend to about 12,000 feet (3,700 m). It shines with a bright green bioluminescence made by photophore organs that emit light. This small shark grows 20 inches (50 cm) long at most, but its razor-sharp teeth bite chunks out of much larger prey, leaving cookie-cutter marks on their flesh.

Suckers and ink

The soft-bodied cuttlefish aggressively catches prey with sucker pads at the end of its two tentacles. With these, it pushes fish and crustaceans into its sharp beak. The cuttlefish changes color to camouflage itself. It squirts dark ink at predators and flashes bright colors during fights.

Two tentacles
Gas-filled bone
Beak
Ink sac
Eight arms near the mouth

79

Deep-sea Discoveries

The life forms of the midnight zone are continually under investigation. Scientists lower special traps that delicately lift up tender creatures without damaging them. They also observe microscopic organisms that feed and breathe by chemosynthesis—absorbing chemicals from the water.

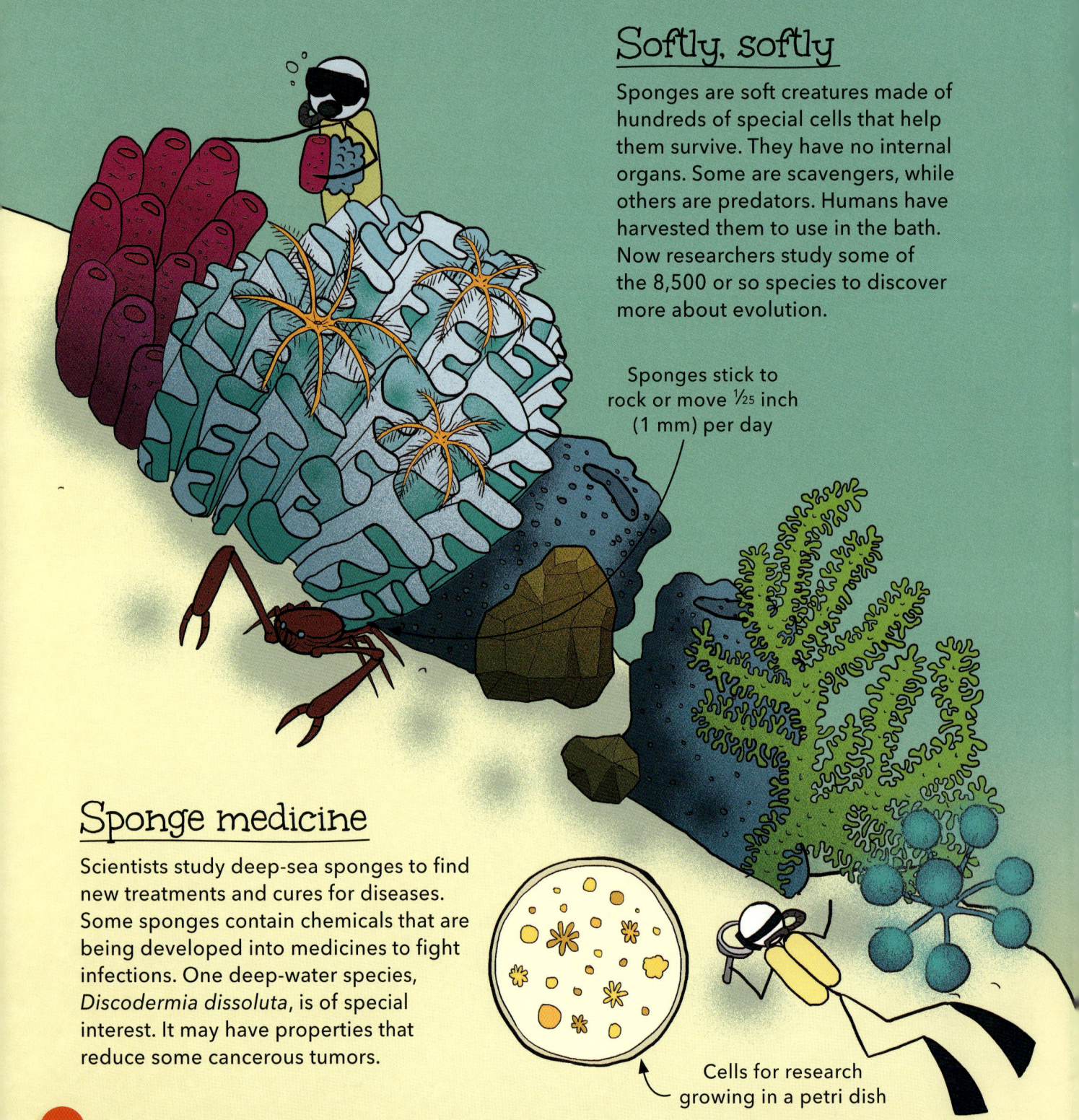

Softly, softly

Sponges are soft creatures made of hundreds of special cells that help them survive. They have no internal organs. Some are scavengers, while others are predators. Humans have harvested them to use in the bath. Now researchers study some of the 8,500 or so species to discover more about evolution.

Sponges stick to rock or move 1/25 inch (1 mm) per day

Sponge medicine

Scientists study deep-sea sponges to find new treatments and cures for diseases. Some sponges contain chemicals that are being developed into medicines to fight infections. One deep-water species, *Discodermia dissoluta*, is of special interest. It may have properties that reduce some cancerous tumors.

Cells for research growing in a petri dish

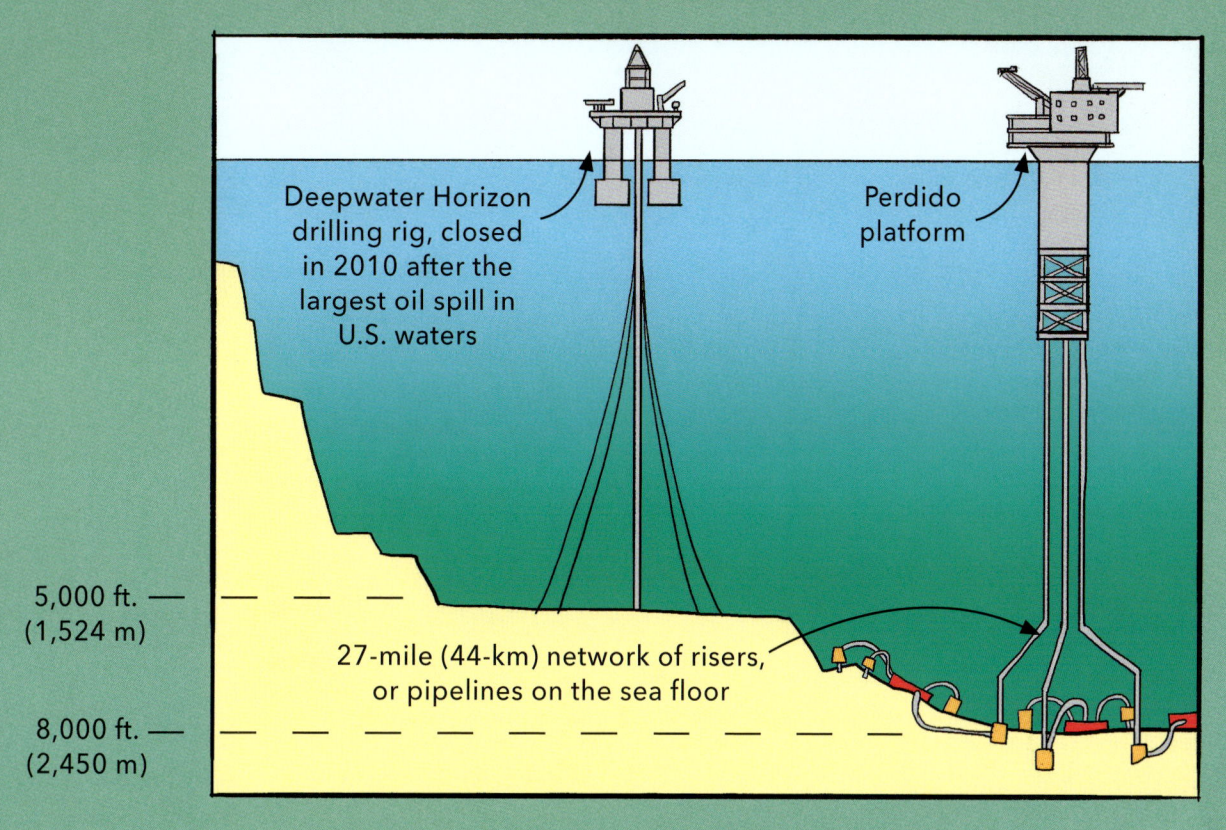

Deepwater Horizon drilling rig, closed in 2010 after the largest oil spill in U.S. waters

Perdido platform

5,000 ft. (1,524 m)

27-mile (44-km) network of risers, or pipelines on the sea floor

8,000 ft. (2,450 m)

Deepest well

In the Gulf of Mexico, Perdido platform sits in 8,000 feet (2,450 m) of water above the deepest oil and gas well, which was drilled 1.9 miles (3 km) into the seabed. *Perdido* means "lost" in Spanish.

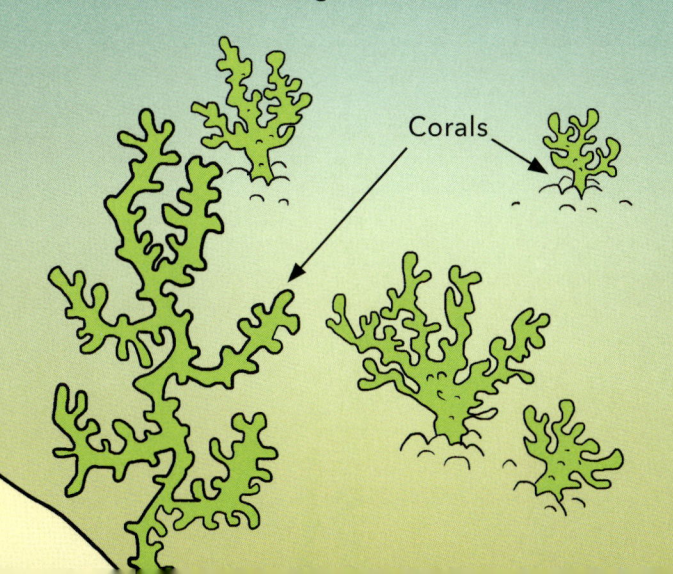

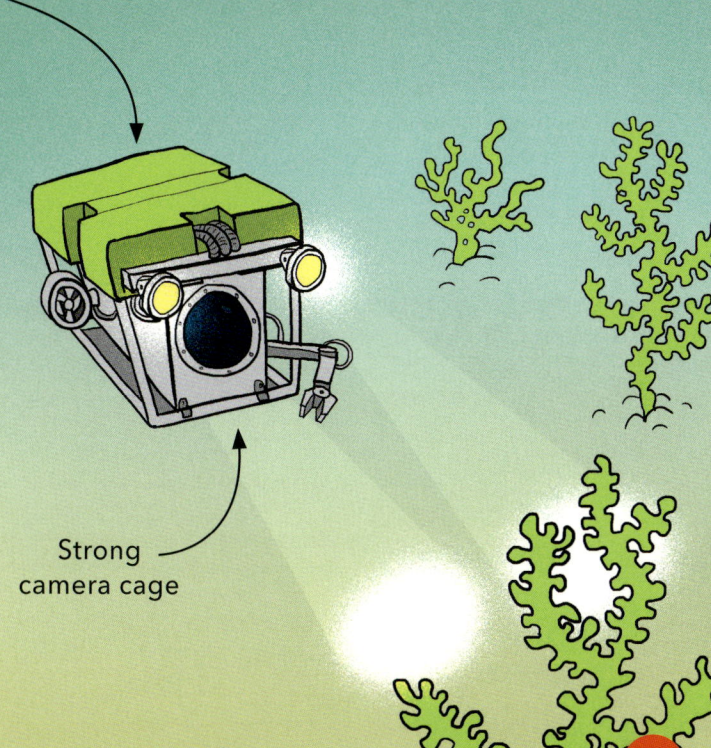

Photo shoot

Remote-control cameras that withstand enormous water pressure capture images of coral gardens. Corals are important habitats for other life-forms and can be indicators of climate change. More than 4,800 coral species have been found so far, over half of these in the deep sea. Some are as tiny as a small seed, while others grow as tall as a house.

Corals

Strong camera cage

Temperature:
122–752°F
(50–400°C)

Smoking chimneys

Hydrothermal vents form on the ocean floor above hot moving magma. Cracks in the floor let seawater seep in. This water is heated by the magma and bubbles up again. The boiling water brings with it dissolved rock minerals that harden into a crust, which builds up into chimneys.

Hydrothermal plume containing oxygen, sulfur, or acids

Hydrothermal vent

Polychaete worm with bristly body segments

Chilled out

In the Gulf of Mexico and away from the warm vents, a species of polychaete worm, or bristle worm, lives in chilly methane ice burrows.

The Black Abyss

The abyss is mostly a pitch black, icy zone, but life still exists here. And where the ocean floor lies close to inner Earth's hot magma, hydrothermal vents occur. Discovered only in 1977, these vents teem with creatures that, amazingly, survive the most hostile conditions.

Frilled shark

The frilled shark is rarely seen, but we know that its eel-like body is about 6 feet (1.8 m) long. It catches prey half its size with 300 needlelike teeth. It is named after the six frill-like gill slits at the sides of its head, through which it receives oxygen.

Frilly gill slits

Dead vent

Stalked jellyfish

See-through creatures

Normally, translucent stalked jellyfish, or "stauromedusae," live mostly near the shore, but new species have been found clustering around dead hydrothermal vents. Stalked jellyfish move slowly, just shifting their position slightly. They are hard to see, because their color is adapted to blend in with their habitat.

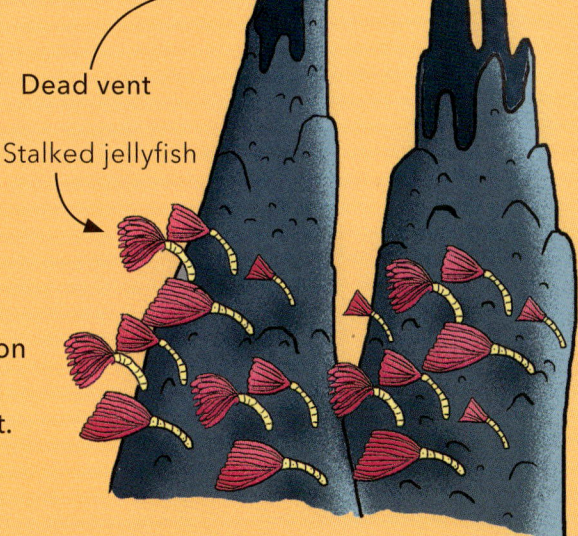

Giant tube worms

These bright red, translucent creatures live around the chimneys of warm hydrothermal vents. They have no eyes, mouth, or stomach. Tube worms use energy passed down by bacteria that live on them. The bacteria take in the chemical hydrogen sulfide from the vent, and it keeps the tube worms alive. In turn, the bacteria live on blood produced by the tube worms.

Tube worm's blood gives it a red color

83

Secrets of the Abyss

To explore the abyss, scientists use state-of-the-art technology to map its hidden crevices, monitor important global currents, and look for new marine species. The discovery of hydrothermal vents (see pages 20–21) also revealed deposits of precious minerals, such as cobalt and gold.

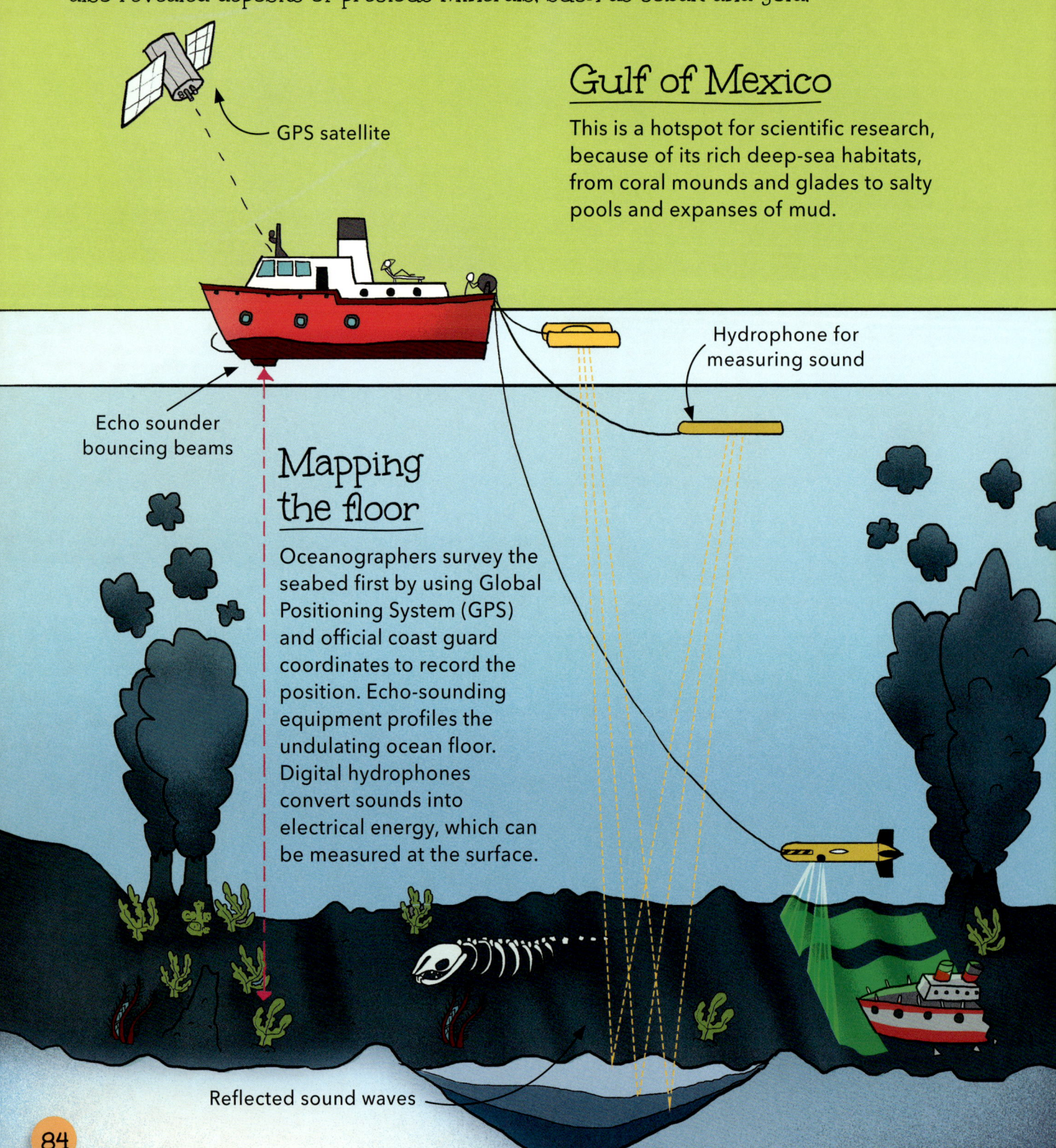

GPS satellite

Gulf of Mexico

This is a hotspot for scientific research, because of its rich deep-sea habitats, from coral mounds and glades to salty pools and expanses of mud.

Echo sounder bouncing beams

Hydrophone for measuring sound

Mapping the floor

Oceanographers survey the seabed first by using Global Positioning System (GPS) and official coast guard coordinates to record the position. Echo-sounding equipment profiles the undulating ocean floor. Digital hydrophones convert sounds into electrical energy, which can be measured at the surface.

Reflected sound waves

84

Underwater robotics

Robotic submarines, which are controlled from the surface, explore and record conditions in the abyss. Some grab samples to bring up for research. Others use fiber-optic technology to capture 3D videos and still images. Microphones pick up such sounds as whale song and volcanic eruptions on the ocean floor.

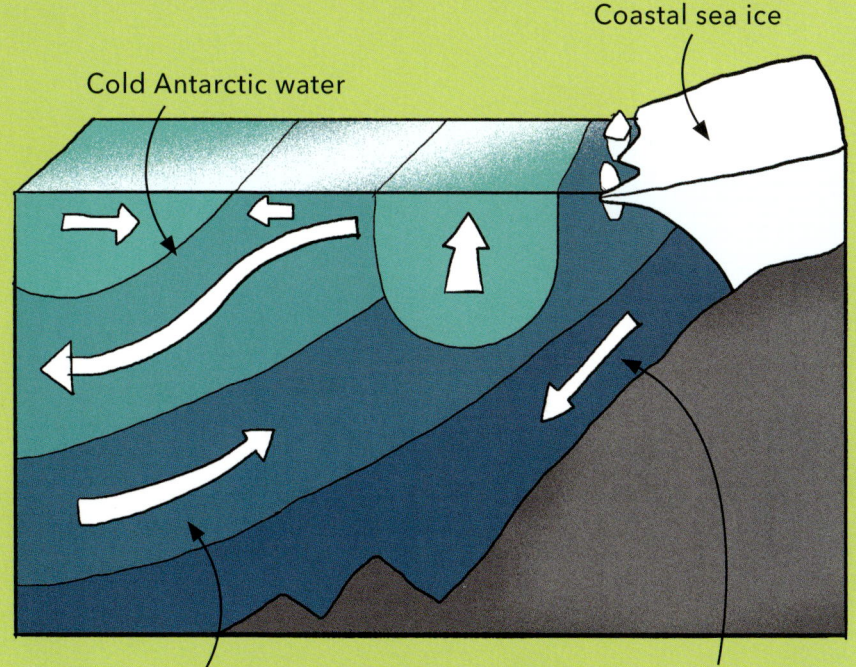

Boom arms for grabbers and instruments

Currents

Oceanographers observe deep-sea currents closely, because their movement, temperature, and salt content give clues to climate change. The Antarctic Circumpolar Current begins with freezing, dense salty water sinking, jump-starting movement in this zone. It meets and mixes with warmer water and flows to other regions.

Cold Antarctic water

Coastal sea ice

Warm subtropical water

Cold salty water sinking

Useful venom

Scientists are looking deeper for new species that may have unexpected benefits for humans. The cone snail's lethal venom contains a wide range of chemicals that are being developed into medicines, including painkillers. The creature's powerful poison is unleashed through a long tongue called a proboscis.

Proboscis with venom

85

The Ocean's Trenches

Ocean floors rise and fall with Earth's highest mountains and deepest valleys, or trenches. These can plunge 5–6 miles (8–10 km) down and are slightly warmer than the abyss above. Their habitats are rocky, although soft sediment lies in the bottom of some trenches.

No buoyancy swim bladder

Translucent fish

V-shape trench

Trench formation

Most trenches have a V shape and are formed where one oceanic plate slides beneath another. Volcanic islands often lie around a trench's rim.

Under pressure

Water pressure in the trenches is extreme. The gas-filled swim bladder that gives a fish buoyancy is not present in many deep-sea species. Instead these fish produce heavy concentrations of a chemical that helps the body's cells withstand pressure.

Volcanoes

Strings of underwater volcanoes run for miles on the deep-ocean floor. In 2011, sonar images captured the Tonga Trench as it swallowed giant volcanoes into its depths. This trench is an active fault line that runs north of New Zealand toward the small islands of Tonga and Samoa in the South Pacific Ocean. It reaches 6¾ miles (10.9 km) down at its deepest.

Trench fish

Delicate, translucent snailfish survive the depths of the trenches. In 2014, a new species was discovered 5 miles (8 km) down in the Mariana Trench. This snailfish has a dog-shaped head and its fins are broad. Scientists believe the sensors that cover the fins detect prey in the soft mud.

Snailfish with broad fins

Mariana Trench

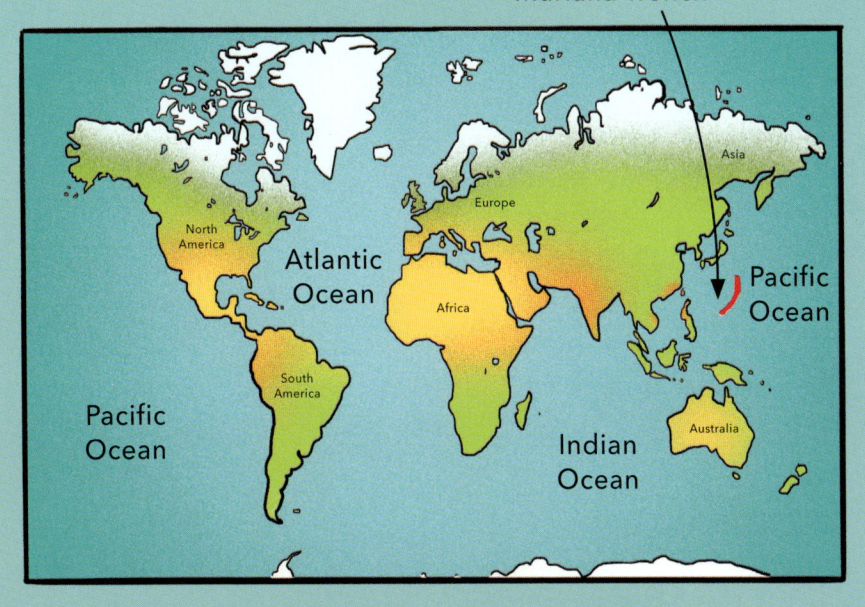

Deep, deeper . . .

The Mariana Trench is the deepest in our oceans. Its lowest point is the Challenger Deep, nearly 7 miles (11 km) down. In 2005, scientists examined samples from its soil. They were surprised to find the single-celled "foraminifera" organism, which has a soft shell, living so deep down. It is normally found in the layers above.

North America
Atlantic Ocean
Europe
Asia
Africa
Pacific Ocean
South America
Indian Ocean
Australia
Pacific Ocean

87

Taking the Plunge

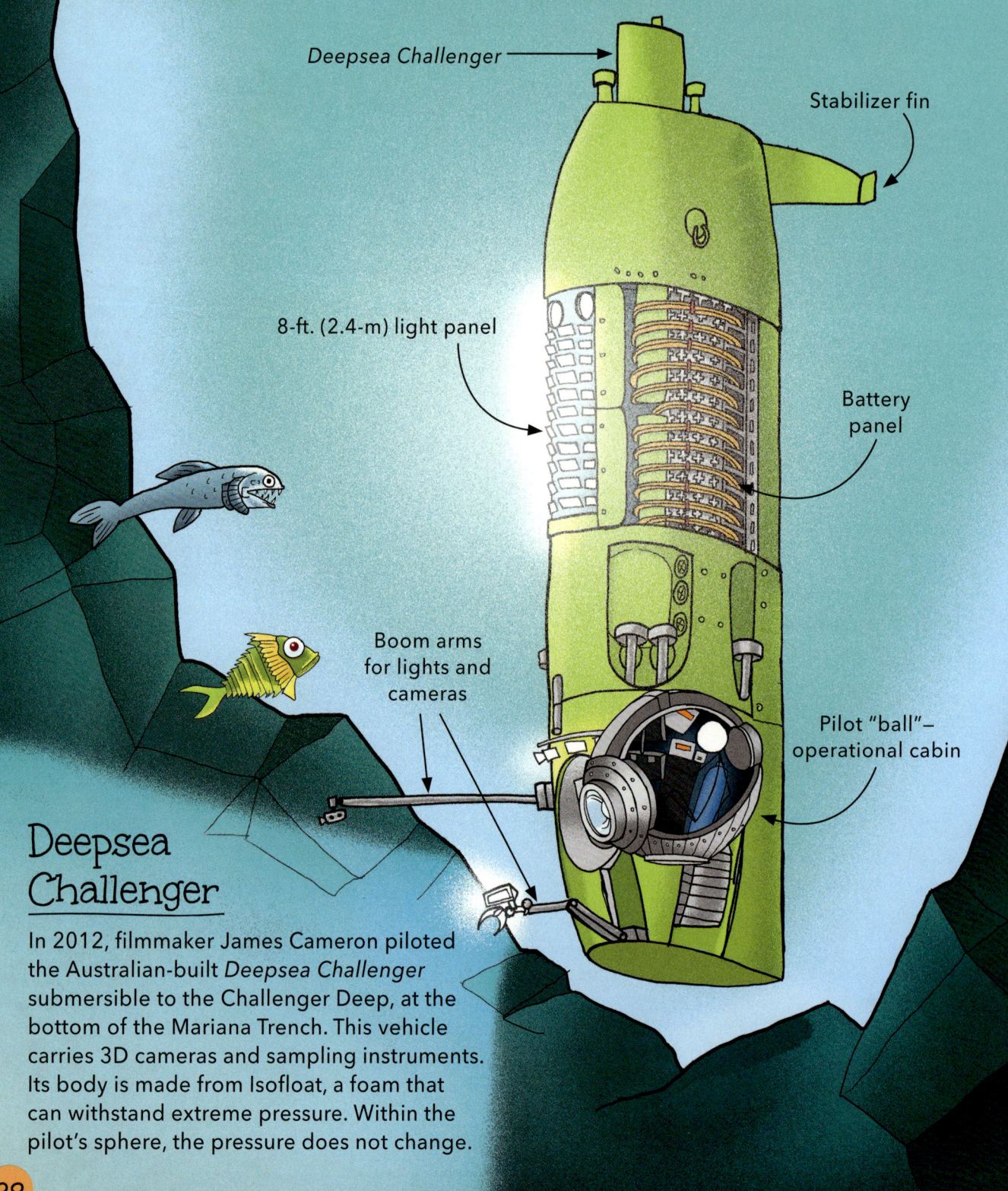

The trenches are an exciting wilderness for scientists to explore, but conditions are tough. Equipment has to cope with a weight of water almost as heavy as 50 jumbo jets. Research has to be carefully managed so that habitats are not destroyed.

Deepsea Challenger

Stabilizer fin

8-ft. (2.4-m) light panel

Battery panel

Boom arms for lights and cameras

Pilot "ball"– operational cabin

Deepsea Challenger

In 2012, filmmaker James Cameron piloted the Australian-built *Deepsea Challenger* submersible to the Challenger Deep, at the bottom of the Mariana Trench. This vehicle carries 3D cameras and sampling instruments. Its body is made from Isofloat, a foam that can withstand extreme pressure. Within the pilot's sphere, the pressure does not change.

Mapping the trenches

Echo sounding maps the shape of our deeply plunging seabed. Echo sounders work by reflecting sound waves off the bottom. The waves' lengths show the rise and fall of the ocean floor. Echo sounding was first used in 1920 by German physicist Alexander Behm (1880–1952).

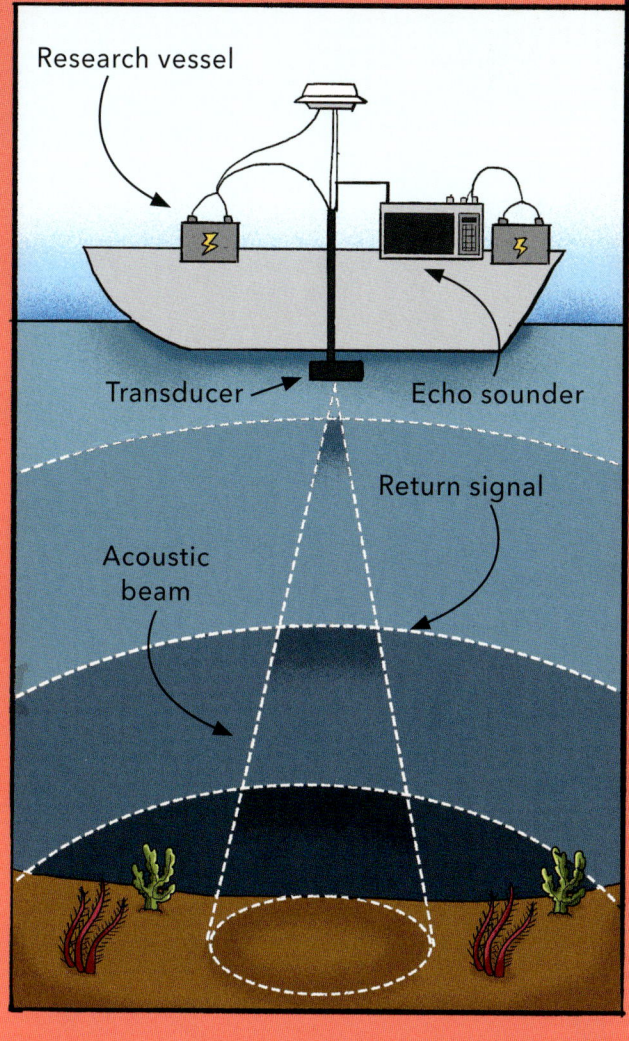

Research vessel

Transducer

Echo sounder

Return signal

Acoustic beam

Infrared LED illuminators

ORCA camera

Deep down this "Eye-in-the-Sea" illuminates the image in front of it using powerful red lights that most creatures in this zone cannot see.

Tracking earthquakes

The trenches help us to find ways of monitoring earth tremors. Hydrophone instruments (example right) are lowered into the trench. These measure the pressure from any movement in the trench floor. The hydrophones' transponders (the yellow spheres) convert the movements into electrical signals that are analyzed at the surface.

Transponder

The Center of Earth

Earth's core lies deep beneath the molten mantle and crusty lithosphere. The outer edge of the core is nearly 1,860 miles (3,000 km) from the surface, while its center is more than 3,700 miles (6,000 km) away. The core's temperature can reach 10,832°F (6000°C).

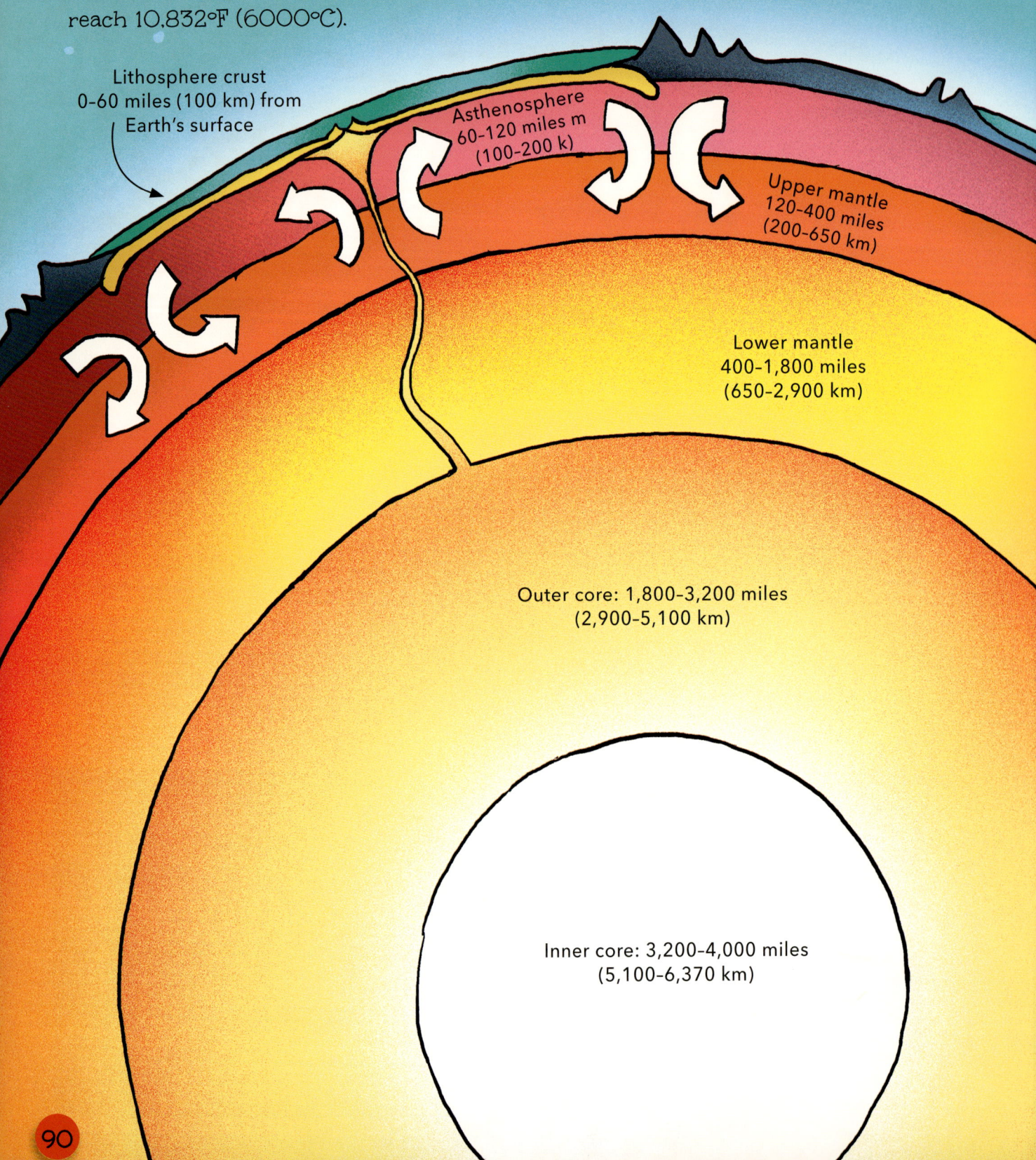

Lithosphere crust
0–60 miles (100 km) from Earth's surface

Asthenosphere
60–120 miles m
(100–200 k)

Upper mantle
120–400 miles
(200–650 km)

Lower mantle
400–1,800 miles
(650–2,900 km)

Outer core: 1,800–3,200 miles
(2,900–5,100 km)

Inner core: 3,200–4,000 miles
(5,100–6,370 km)

Earth's magnetic force

The planet's outer core is liquid but the inner core mainly consists of solid iron. Billions of years ago this iron was molten and squeezed down into the center, where it hardened. The movement of molten iron around the hard core creates an electric current, which in turn generates a magnetic field.

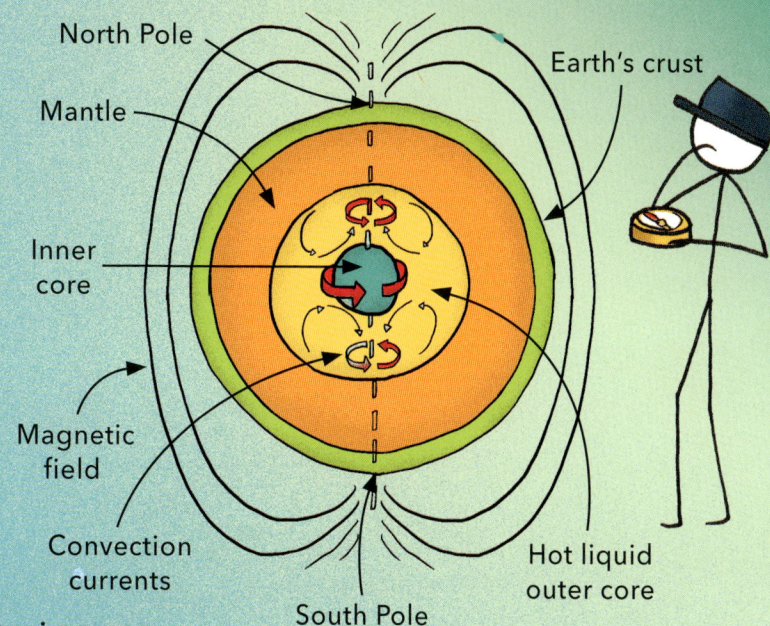

North Pole
Earth's crust
Mantle
Inner core
Magnetic field
Convection currents
South Pole
Hot liquid outer core

Core science

For more than 100 years, scientists have studied the texture of Earth's core by measuring energy waves from earth tremors. At first, scientists used seismometers to follow the paths of the S (secondary) waves. But these could not reach Earth's solid inner core. In the 1930s, scientist Inge Lehmann discovered a new P (primary) wave that passed through the entire core, so registering both its layers.

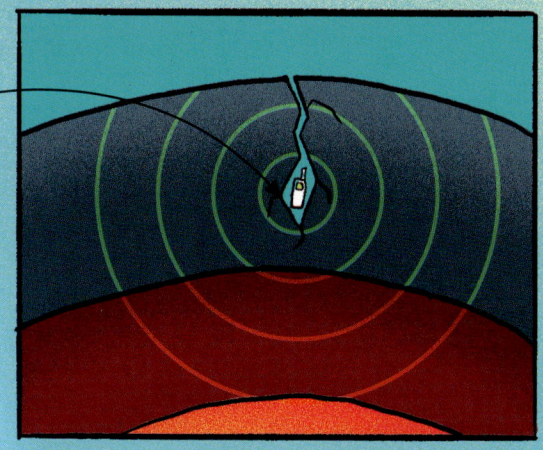

Seismometer measuring waves from tremor

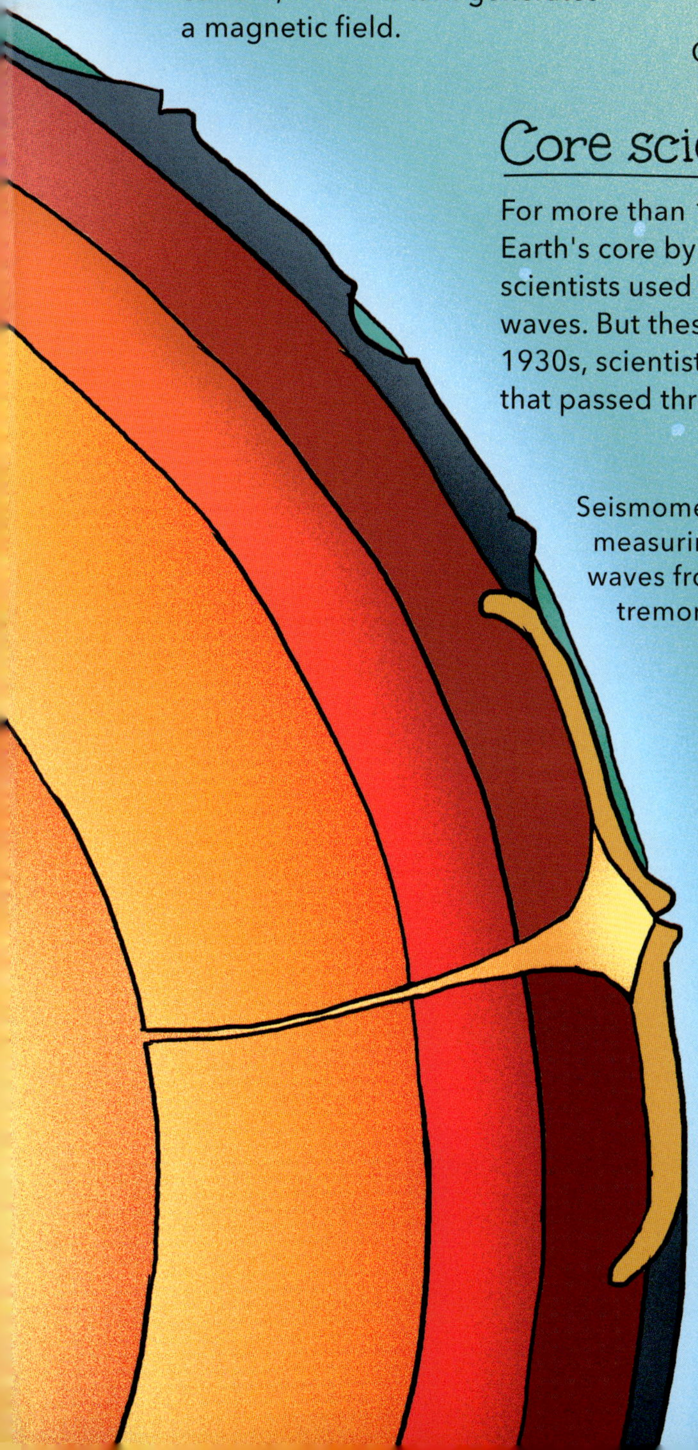

What we know so far

The liquid outer core is made mostly of iron, with some nickel and oxygen gas. We do not know how hot it is, because it moves up and down, which varies the temperature. Although the hard inner core is made mostly of iron, it may contain nickel, too. At its outer edge, the inner core freezes, chilling the liquid outer core next to it. It hardens, which means that the inner core is growing at about 1/50 inch (0.5 mm) each year.

INDEX

A
above ground 48, 58–61
abyss 68, 82–85
air pressure 27
airglow 17
alpine layer 32, 33
anemometers 26
anglerfish 75
astronauts 13
Attwater's prairie chickens 37
avalanches 33

B
barometers 27
bioluminescent light 75, 78, 79
birds 35, 37, 41
black bears 13
blobfish 78
blue jets 18
bristle worms 82

C
cables 55, 68, 69
canyons 40, 41
carbon sinks 76
cargo ships 73
cavity flooring 59
ceilometers 26
chlorofluorocarbons (CFCs) 21
climate change 25
clouds 17, 19, 23, 25, 26
coffee 34
cone snails 85
continental slope 74
coral 70, 81
crustaceans 74
currents 85
cuttlefish 79

D
department stores 58
deep-sea diving 77
Deepsea Challenger 88
diamonds 43
Dobsonmeter 21
double-decker trains 66

E
earthquakes 46, 47
Earth's core 90, 91
echo sounding 84, 89
echolocation 75
elevators 54, 55
exosphere 6, 8–11
explorers 77

F
fatbergs 64
filming underwater 76, 81, 88
fishing 72
flood danger 61, 64
foundations 68, 69

G
glaciers 30, 38
gases 9, 12, 16, 21, 22,
geocorona 9
giant squid 75, 76
Global Positioning System (GPS) 10
gold mining 42, 43
grasscrete 61
Gulf of Mexico 81, 82, 84

H
helipads 51
Himalayan Snowcock 50
Hubble Space Telescope 13, 14, 15
human activity 52
humidity 27
hurricanes 24–25
hydroelectric power (HEP) 30
hydrophones 84, 89
hydrothermal vents 82, 84
hygrometers 27

I
International Space Station (ISS) 12, 13

J
jet aircraft 19

L
lakes 33
lichens 31
lighting 57
living walls 60

M
magnetic field 49
mammals 32, 35, 37
mapping 89
Mariana Trench 87
Mars 30
medicines 80, 85
mesosphere 6, 16, 17
midnight zone 68, 78–81
mining 42, 43
montane layer 34, 35
mountaineering 31

N
neon lights 57
noise reduction 59, 61

O
oceanography 77, 84, 85
oil 73, 81
oil and gas extraction 36, 43
open-plan offices 59
optical fibers 62
ORCA cameras 89
oxygen levels 23
ozone layer 20, 21

P
phytoplankton 71
plains 36, 37
plants 33, 34, 38
plastic trash 72
power
　high 48, 54, 55
　underground 62, 63

R
rain making 25
red elves 16, 17
reptiles 41

rivers 30, 38, 39, 40
robotic submarines 85
rock art 40
roller coasters 53
rooftops 48, 50-53

S
salmon 39
satellites 10, 11, 25
screens 57
sea cucumbers 78
seaweeds 70
sewers 64, 65
sharks 85, 83
skyscrapers 48, 50-53
snailfish 87
snow dogs 50
snow leopards 32
snowy peaks 30, 31
solar panels 50
sounding rockets 8
Southern Pinwheel galaxy 15
space shuttle 13
spiders 30
sponges 80
sports 33, 52
sprites and elves 17

storms 24, 25, 29
stalked jellyfish 83
stratosphere 6, 18-19
streetcars 61
street life 60, 63
subways 66, 67
sun 9, 30
sunlight zone 68, 70-73

T
Tambora eruption 45
tectonic plates 46, 47
telecommunications equipment 50
termites 37
thermometers 27
thermosphere 6, 12-15
tiltmeters 45
tornadoes 24, 25, 29
travel underground 66, 67
troposphere 6, 22-27
toxic gases 45
travel 39
trees 32, 34, 35
trenches 68, 86-89
tsunamis 49
tube worms 83
tunnel boring machines (TBMs) 67
twilight zone 68, 74-77

U
ultraviolet (UV) rays 9, 15, 20
underground 48, 62-68

V
valley floor 38, 39
volcanoes 44, 43, 87

W
water 64, 65
water cycle 23
weather balloons 19
weather data 19, 26, 27
whales 71, 75
wind 50
wind speeds 26
wind turbines 51
wiring 56
workspaces 58, 59

X
X-15 rocket plane 13

Z
zooplankton 71

The Author
Catherine Chambers was born in Adelaide, South Australia, grew up in the UK, and studied African History and Swahili at the School of Oriental and African Studies in London. She has written about 130 books for children and young adults, and enjoys seeking out intriguing facts for her nonfiction titles, which cover history, cultures, faiths, biography, geography, and the environment.

The Illustrator
John Paul has a BSc in Biology from the University of Sussex, UK, and a graduate certificate in animation from the University of the West of England. He devotes his spare time to growing chili peppers, perfecting his plan for a sustainable future, and caring for a small plastic dinosaur. He has three pet squid that live in a bathtub, which makes drawing in ink economical.

Picture Credits (abbreviations: t = top; b = bottom; c = center; l = left; r = right)
15 tr NASA, ESA, and the Hubble Heritage Team (STScI/AURA)

Every effort has been made to trace the copyright holders. And we acknowledge in advance any unintentional omissions. We would be pleased to insert the appropriate acknowledgment in any subsequent publication